Social Justice
and the Churches

Text copyright © 2014 remains with the authors and for the collection with ATF Theology. All rights reserved. Except for any fair dealing permitted under the Copyright Act, no part of the publication may be reproduced by any means without prior permission. Inquiries should be made in the first instance with the publisher.

A Forum for Theology in the World
Volume 1, Issue 2, 2014

A Forum for Theology in the World is an academic refereed journal aimed at engaging with issues in the contemporary world, a world which is pluralist and eucumenical in nature. The journal reflects this pluralism and ecumenism. Each edition is theme specific and has its own editor responsible for the production. The journal aims to elicit and encourage dialogue on topics and issues in contemporary society and within a variety of religious traditions. The Editor in Chief welcomes submissions of manuscripts, collections of articles, for review from individuals or institutions, which may be from seminars or conferences or written specifically for the journal. An internal peer review is expected before submitting the manuscript. It is the expectation of the publisher that, once a manuscript has been accepted for publication, it will be submitted according to the house style to be found at the back of this volume. All submissions to the Editor in Chief are to be sent to: hdregan@atf.org.au.

Each edition is available as a journal subscription, or as a book in print, pdf or epub, through the ATF Press web site — www.atfpress.com. Journal subscriptions are also available through EBSCO and other library suppliers.

Editor in Chief
Hilary Regan, ATF Press

A Forum for Theology in the World is published by ATF Theology and imprint of
ATF (Australia) Ltd (ABN 90 116 359 963) and
is published twice or three times a year.
ISSN 1329-6264

ATF Press
PO Box 504
Hindmarsh SA 5007
Australia
www.atfpress.com

Subscription Rates 2014

Print	On-Line	Print and On-line
Aust $65 Individuals	Aus $55 individuals	Aus $75 individuals
Aus $90 Institutions	Aus $80 individuals	Aus $100 instiutions

Social Justice and the Churches: Challenges and Responsibilities

edited by John D'Arcy May

ATF Theology
Adelaide
2014

Forum for Theology in the World Vol 1 No 2/2014

Contents

Introduction
    John D'Arcy May — vii

1 Key Challenges and Responsibilities of the Churches in the Current Social and Cultural Context
    Frank Brennan — 1

2 The Salvation Army and Social Commitment
    Jenny Begent — 35

3 Social Concern and Vatican II: A Response from the Catholic Tradition
    Max Vodola — 45

4 Social Thinking Among Churches of Christ in Australia
    Gerald Rose — 55

5 Social Concern in the Baptist Tradition
    Geoff Pound — 73

6 Anglican Social Thinking for Australia: Making a Difference?
    Ray Cleary — 89

7 Social Concern in the Tradition of the Uniting Church in Australia
    Mark Zirnsak — 113

8 Social justice in the Coptic Orthodox Church
    Shenouda Boutros — 131

9 The Importance of Knowing Our Christian Social Traditions
   Margaret Coffey   141

Contributors   151

Forum for Theology in the World Vol 1 No 2/2014

Introduction
Making A Difference: A Rhetorical Question?

John D'Arcy May

Several contributors to the symposium of the Yarra Institute for Religion and Social Policy on 'Christian Social Thinking for Australia: making a difference?' commented that the title was surely a rhetorical question: of course the churches make a difference in the social sphere. But as the very different contributions by speakers from seven Christian traditions were presented, an undertone of frustration also became evident: that one's church was *not allowed* to make a difference because of the current legislative and political constellation, or that one was *not able* to make a difference because of the way one's church was constituted. Far from being a rather boring repetition of the well-known and well-worn principles that are supposedly common to all traditions, the papers were startlingly distinctive in their approaches, demonstrating that there is a wealth of social justice resources for Christians to draw on if only they were better informed about one another's starting points. It was this, perhaps, that was the main benefit of the conference: that representatives of each of these seven traditions, possibly for the first time, were able to hear well-informed accounts of the social justice perspectives of all the others.

There was a certain Catholic bias in the design of the conference, in that Professor Frank Brennan, the well-known Jesuit legal scholar and human rights advocate, initiated the proceedings with a very substantial and wide-ranging examination of some of the most controversial social justice issues at present being discussed in Australia. He exploited to the full what has rapidly become known as the 'Francis effect' since the new pope began not only speaking frankly about the priorities in Catholic social justice discourse but bearing witness to it in his own lifestyle. Acknowledging that his expertise is in law rather than economics, Brennan went on to offer genuinely new and controversial insights in areas such as the abortion debate, the question of discrimination on grounds of sexual orientation or religious affiliation, the legal position on vilification because of race or religion, the possibility of incorporating elements of Sharia law into Western jurisprudence, the status of same-sex marriage and civil unions, and the controversies over asylum seekers and border protection, each time with reasoned legal argument (some of which had to be omitted here for reasons of space). This left the participants with a lot to digest, though some took up Brennan's points and begged to differ.

Fr Max Vodola expanded on Brennan's concluding salute to the sources of Catholic social teaching by treating in more detail the long tradition of social encyclicals. He did not dodge the issue of a certain discrepancy between style and substance in this tradition, made manifest in the fresh approach of Pope Francis and reaching crisis proportions in the sexual abuse scandals which have been revealed in recent years.

As Margaret Coffey remarks in her concluding reflections, a number of contributions are in marked contrast to this Catholic tradition of authoritative teaching and doctrinal continuity. Revd Gerald Rose explains how the Churches of Christ owe allegiance to the 'radical left wing of Protestantism', jealously preserving a congregational structure with no central authority. Thomas and Alexander Campbell saw themselves as initiating a 'restoration movement' to retrieve the 'primitive faith of the New Testament'. Problems arise when political involvement is called for: the social ethic that emerges is orientated to the personal experience of the individual rather than the rational authority of a tradition, so that maintaining moral standards in the wider society becomes a problem rather than a programme.

Revd Geoff Pound portrays the Baptist heritage in similar vein: stemming from the Free Church tradition, in a sense separatist and hence more comfortable *outside* social structures and state allegiances. Yet he also envisages a 'public theology' which is not averse to participating in the pluralism of the public square.

The Anglican Church, too, as Revd Ray Cleary points out, has no central *magisterium* which could presuppose or bring about a consensus on social or doctrinal matters. As a former chief executive of Anglicare he is aware that such agencies arose from outreach initiatives at parish level, not from the prioritising of social justice issues by the Church; indeed, he suspects that such issues are regarded as secondary in ecclesiastical circles. For him this relationship needs to be rethought, for here lies the Church's real mission. Anglicans must learn to deploy the language of faith in such a way that it has an impact in pluralist societies.

The Uniting Church, a much more recent foundation (1977), has made social concern central to its constitution and has appropriated the Catholic notion of subsidiarity. Revd Mark Zirnsak, more than any other contributor, offers detailed analysis of economic incongruities such as tax evasion in a taxation system skewed in favour of the rich – including the media moguls who can influence political opinion in this sense. He takes issue with Frank Brennan on a number of questions and explicitly mentions the potential of ecumenical co-operation in resolving disagreements among Christians.

Major Jenny Begent of the Salvation Army offers yet another perspective on combating social inequality, speaking frankly about the conflicts this entails for an organisation that fought free of established churches in order better to serve the poor, but has inexorably succumbed to the pressures of institutionalisation. It was founded on the premise that 'there is no improving the future without disturbing the present' (Catherine Booth), but it does not always succeed in being a prophetic presence, holding together evangelism and social service.

An entirely different but equally valuable perspective is provided by Fr Boutros Shenouda of the Coptic Orthodox Church. Although it enjoys a long tradition of social activism, which it continues in Australia with a range of services, this Church is continually aware of the persecution its members have suffered for many centuries in Egypt, perhaps never more than in recent years, when the attempt was made to apply Sharia law to the whole society. He too takes issue with Frank Brennan on matters such as same-sex marriage, noting that Christian opinion, once fairly uniform, has now diverged markedly.

At least two questions of fundamental importance emerge from this very fruitful discussion. One is the classical sociological tenet formulated by Max Weber as the institutionalisation of charism: if a movement brought into being by an inspired founder is to survive, certain compromises must be struck with the structures and norms of a society it may have set out to oppose. In this inevitable process there is both profit and loss, as the early history of Christianity itself instantiates. Another question is that of the relationship between ecclesiology and social ethics. Although the Catholic Church's coherent body of social teaching may give this impression, the principles of social justice do not exist in a vacuum; they are not given *a priori* as abstractions which may be 'applied' as circumstances require. Each church has its own founding narrative, its own context of origin, and these determine the extent to which society with its economic and political structures is accepted or rejected in any given situation. Margaret Coffey's reference to Frederick Ozanam and his Society of St Vincent de Paul in the context of nineteenth-century French Catholicism illustrates this nicely. If the conference did anything, it brought such questions to the fore and made Christians committed to social justice more aware of their different responses to them. This diversity need not mean dissipation of resources; it could equally encourage mutual enrichment and support.

The conference, held in the Oratory of Newman College in the University of Melbourne, was organised by the Yarra Institute for Religion and Social Policy, whose Director, Fr Bruce Duncan CSsR, played a major role in recruiting the speakers and initiating this publication. We also wish to thank Anne Doyle for her splendid proof-reading and support.

Forum for Theology in the World Vol 1 No 2/2014

Key Challenges and Responsibilities of the Churches in the Current Social and Cultural Context

Frank Brennan

Address to the Yarra Institute for Religion and Social Policy, in the Oratory, Newman College, University of Melbourne, 8 November 2013

The challenge

I am honoured to accept the invitation from the Yarra Institute for Religion and Social Policy to deliver the keynote address of this conference on Christian social thinking. You have gathered to ask the hopefully rhetorical and self-evident question whether you are making a difference. Fr Bruce Duncan, Director of the Institute, has asked me to address 'the challenges and responsibilities of the churches in the current social, ecumenical and cultural context, especially about engaging positively in helping promote human wellbeing in Australia and beyond.' Tomorrow seven representatives of various Christian denominations will respond to my remarks in the light of their social tradition, identifying what is specific to it, and how their tradition could best contribute to a fairer and more inclusive society. I will of course speak largely from my own experience and tradition which is Catholic and Jesuit. I have one major reservation about undertaking this task. My training is in law; I know little about economics. Sadly, I think the Christian churches are all but absent from the economic debate other than making the occasional, predictable utterance about ensuring that no one is left worse off as the result of new policy measures.

Ahead of me is a generation of Australian Jesuits who dedicated the prime of their lives with chalk dust teaching schoolboys to be generous and not to count the cost, to fight and not to heed the wounds, to toil and not to seek for rest, to labour and not to ask reward save that of knowing that they do the Lord's holy will. In an age when religious faith and observance are fragile, these Jesuits have justifiably taken pride in alumni who have persevered in faith, hope and love. They have also taken delight in those alumni who have dedicated themselves to lives of service in the Church and in the professions and in providing assistance to the poor and marginalised. For the moment that generation of Jesuit teachers enjoys the fruits of their educational labours, seeing Jesuit alumni on the national stage of public service as prime minister, chief justice, leader of the opposition, treasurer, minister for education and minister for agriculture.

But there is no cause for triumphalism. I remember when there was a handful of Jesuit alumni in John Howard's first ministry. I told my fellow Jesuits that the Aborigines and refugees amongst whom I worked regarded the Howard government as the toughest with which they had ever had to deal. Training in Christian social teaching does not necessarily displace class interest, national interest or personal preference. Our challenge always is to assist society's decision makers to form their consciences, inform their consciences and to those consciences be true, including the discharge of all appropriate obligations of political life including attention to the electorate's wishes, party policy, and the national interest.

Our context — a contemporary Catholic perspective

I have been overwhelmed by the positive response by all sorts of people to the election of the first Jesuit pope. I have happily received the congratulations without quite knowing what to do with them, nor what I did to deserve them! It's still early days in his pontificate, but I think he has opened up a vast new panacea and not just for Catholics. Francis is theologically orthodox, politically conservative, comfortable in his own skin, infectiously pastoral, and truly committed to the poor. Of late, most thinking Catholics engaged in the world have wondered how you could possibly be theologically orthodox and infectiously pastoral at the one time, how you could be politically conservative and still have a commitment to the poor, how you could be comfortable in your own skin—at ease in church and in the public square, equally comfortable and uncomfortable in conversation with fawning devotees and hostile critics. Think only of Francis's remark during the press conference on the plane on the way back from World Youth Day: 'If a person is gay and seeks the Lord and has good will, who am I to judge him?' Gone are the days of rainbow sashes outside Cathedrals and threats of communion bans.

As Francis says in the lengthy interview he did for the Jesuit journal *La Civiltà Cattolica* in September 2013:

> We need to proclaim the Gospel on every street corner, preaching the good news of the kingdom and healing, even with our preaching, every kind of disease and wound. In Buenos Aires I used to receive letters from homosexual persons who are 'socially wounded' because they tell me that they feel like the church has always condemned them

In that interview he recalls:

> A person once asked me, in a provocative manner, if I approved of homosexuality. I replied with another question: 'Tell me: when God looks at a gay person, does he endorse the existence of this person with love, or reject and condemn this person?' We must always consider the person. Here we enter into the mystery of the human being. In life, God accompanies persons, and we must accompany them, starting from their situation. It is necessary to accompany them with mercy. When that happens, the Holy Spirit inspires the priest to say the right thing.

Here is a pope who is not just about creating wiggle room or watering down the teachings of the Catholic Church. No, he wants to admit honestly to the world that we hold in tension definitive teachings and pastoral yearnings—held together coherently only by mercy and forgiveness. He explains:

> We cannot insist only on issues related to abortion, gay marriage and the use of contraceptive methods. This is not possible. I have not spoken much about these things, and I was reprimanded for that. But when we speak about these issues, we have to talk about them in a context. The teaching of the church, for that matter, is clear and I am a son of the church, but it is not necessary to talk about these issues all the time. The dogmatic and moral teachings of the church are not all equivalent. The church's pastoral ministry cannot be obsessed with the transmission of a disjointed multitude of doctrines to be imposed insistently. Proclamation in a missionary style focuses on the essentials, on the necessary things: this is also what fascinates and attracts more, what makes the heart burn, as it did for the disciples at Emmaus. We have to find a new balance; otherwise even the moral edifice of the church is likely to fall like a house of cards, losing the freshness and fragrance of the Gospel. The proposal of the Gospel must be more simple, profound, radiant. It is from this proposition that the moral consequences then flow.

If we are honest with ourselves, many of us Catholics have wondered how we can maintain our Christian faith and our commitment at this time in the Catholic Church in the wake of the sexual abuse crisis and the many judgmental utterances about sexuality and reproduction—the church that has spoken longest and loudest about sex in all its modalities seems to be one of the social institutions most needing to get its own house in order in relation to trust, fidelity, love, respect and human dignity. Revelations out of Melbourne and Newcastle and the pending national royal commission hearings leave us with heavy hearts especially about some of our local church leadership before 1996, but we do have a spring in our step that this new Pope, together with rigorous, independent legal processes (even in the face of much media pre-judgment) and local church commitments to transparency and solicitous care of victims, including the establishment of the Truth Justice and Healing Council, provide us with the structures and leadership necessary for 'cooperation, openness, full disclosure and justice for victims and survivors'. The chief Christian paradox is that we are lowly sinners who dare to profess the highest ideals, and that sometimes we cannot do it on our own—we need the help of our critics and the State. Our greatest possibilities are born of the promise of forgiveness and redemption, the hope of new life emerging from suffering and even death. Out of our past failings and our present shame can come future promise and hope.

Let's be in no doubt that the Australian Catholic Church needed help from the State and from civil society so that we might get our house in order in dealing with child abuse which had been occurring at a most unacceptable rate and which had been addressed in too incremental a way. In his essay 'A Catholic Modernity?' Charles Taylor suggests

> In modern, secularist culture there are mingled together both the authentic developments of the Gospel, of an incarnational mode of life, and also a closing off to God that negates the Gospel. The notion is that modern culture, in breaking with the structures and beliefs of Christendom, also carried certain facets of Christian life further than they were ever taken or could have been taken within Christendom. In relation to the earlier forms of Christian culture, we have to face the humbling realisation that the breakout was a necessary condition of the development.

Sometimes it is the State or civil society which provides a corrective or a further spur to the Church to be true to its finest ideals.

Professing religious faith in a secular domain and owning our history

As Christians, we can bring God's blessings to all in our world, even those who have no time for our churches and not much interest in our Lord. Remember how Pope Francis ended his address to the journalists in Rome with a blessing with a difference. He said:

> I told you I was cordially imparting my blessing. Since many of you are not members of the Catholic Church, and others are not believers, I cordially give this blessing silently, to each of you, respecting the conscience of each, but in the knowledge that each of you is a child of God. May God bless you!

Now that's what I call a real blessing for journalists—and not a word of Vaticanese. Respect for the conscience of every person, regardless of their religious beliefs; silence in the face of difference; affirmation of the dignity and blessedness of every person; offering, not coercing; suggesting, not dictating; leaving room for gracious acceptance. These are all good pointers for us Christians helping promote human wellbeing, holding the treasure of Christian tradition, authority and ritual in trust for all the people of God, including children and grandchildren, as we discern how best to make a home for God in our lives and in our world, assured that the Spirit of God has made her home with us.

Religious freedom under the rule of law

Carolyn Evans, Dean of the Melbourne Law School concluded her definitive *Freedom of Religion Under the European Convention on Human Rights* with this observation:

> Religion and belief have been important sources of inspiration for moral and political development, artistic and literary endeavours, and, most importantly, for individuals seeking to live their lives meaningfully and with integrity. Undoubtedly religious freedom has certain social costs and gives rise to the potential to create conflict, but it is nevertheless worthy of far greater protection than it is currently given under the (European) Convention. If religious vitality and tolerance is undermined, European democracy and pluralism will be the weaker for it.

In 2006 Evans joined with Adrienne Stone to convene a conference on law, religion and social change at the Australian National University. The resulting book was published by Cambridge in 2008 with the title, *Law and Religion in Theoretical and Historical Context*. In the introduction, Carolyn noted,

> It was not so long ago that confident predictions were being made about the eventual demise of religion . . . Now, however, religion is back on the public agenda both domestically and internationally. Questions about the role of religion in public life are being prompted by a range of changes in many western states.

Here are a few observations on controversial matters raised in Evans's latest book *Legal Protection of Religious Freedom in Australia* including 'Exemptions from law: conscientious objection to the provision of abortion', 'Non-discrimination laws: friend or foe of religious freedom?', Religious vilification, and the applicability of Sharia law.

Abortion
My views on section 8 of the Abortion Law Reform Act 2008 (Victoria) are well known. Suffice to say I think a legal provision which requires a medical practitioner having a conscientious objection to aborting a post-viable, late-term foetus to refer the mother to another medical practitioner known not to have the same conscientious objection is not only unprincipled; it is unworkable. While such a provision remains on the statute books, it is understandable that some critics of a Charter of Rights and Freedoms authorising such a law regard the Charter as a foil for the soft left political agenda rather than the legal protection for all rights and freedoms, including the freedom of conscience. In an even-handed fashion, Evans describes the views of religious leaders including myself who have spoken of the 'hallmarks of totalitarianism' and then quotes Dr Wendy Larcombe who argued that the provision was relatively inoffensive in that the term 'refer' 'should be understood in its ordinary sense rather than in the medical sense of providing a formal referral'. If that's all it means, why make it a legal requirement? Evans notes,

> Many women's rights groups were concerned that the referral provision was inadequate to protect properly the rights of women who need to access abortions and that the law went too far in protecting religious conscience at the expense of women's health. Both sides of the debate made rights claims and each believed that the law did not adequately protect their legitimate interests.

If the law does not require a formal referral, and if a doctor has a conscientious objection to the deliberate killing of a late-term, viable foetus, why not simply discharge the doctor from any further legal obligation?

Non-discrimination
Church groups in Australia have been engaged in a gruelling campaign to maintain what they regard as justifiable exemptions from the provisions of equal opportunity employment laws. Cardinal Pell makes the point nicely:

> Should the Greens have the right to prefer to employ people who believe in climate change, or should they be forced to employ sceptics? Should Amnesty International have the right to prefer members who are committed to human rights, or should they be forced to accept those who admire dictatorships? Both cases involve discrimination and limiting the freedoms of others, and without it neither organisation would be able to maintain their identity or do their job effectively. Church agencies and schools are not exempt from anti-discrimination law in New South Wales, and the language of 'exemptions' is misleading. Parliaments are obliged by international human rights conventions like the ICCPR to provide protection of religious freedom in any laws which would unfairly restrict the right of religious communities to operate their schools and services in accord with their beliefs and teachings.

While there may be strong agreement about the need to maintain a faith community's right to employ in certain positions only persons who live in conformity with religious teaching, there is plenty of room for disagreement as to how most prudently and charitably to exercise that right. It is not only secularist, anti-church people who think that church organisations and leaders would be displaying homophobia by singling out only gays and lesbians for exclusion from employment in some key positions when heterosexual persons are also living in what the church might formally regard as irregular situations.

During the 2009 National Human Rights Consultation, Bob Carr (ex-Premier from New South Wales) told a conference convened by the Australian Christian Lobby and the Catholic Archdiocese of Melbourne that one of the chief advantages of not having a Charter was that church leaders could deal directly with government. He told the story of the two Archbishops of Sydney coming to see him as premier when there was discussion about a proposed Bill to restrict the freedom of churches to employ only those persons living consistently with church teachings. He was able to give them an immediate assurance that their interests would be protected. It is a matter for prudential political assessment. I think those days have gone. It is a good thing for society that elected political leaders and church leaders are able to meet and talk confidentially. Whatever the situation in the past, it is now not only necessary but also desirable for religious leaders to give a public account of themselves when seeking protection of freedom of religion within appropriate limits, especially when they are in receipt of large government funds for the provision of services to the general community, and not just to members of their faith communities. Religious special exemptions regarding employment are all the more defensible when religious personnel including religious leaders and those with the hands-on directing of religious agencies are prepared to appear before a parliamentary committee and provide a coherent rationale for those exemptions, rather than simply cutting a deal behind closed doors with the premier or prime minister of the day.

Having successfully fought off the prospect of a national human rights Act, 20 key church leaders met with Prime Minister Gillard on 4 April 2011 to plead for freedom to employ in church agencies personnel living and acting in accordance with the religious beliefs of the sponsoring churches. After the meeting, Cardinal Pell briefed the media about the meeting. He was reported in *The Australian* having told Ms Gillard:

> We are very keen to ensure that the right to practise religion in public life continues to be protected in law. It is not ideal that religious freedom is protected by so called 'exemptions and exceptions' in anti-discrimination law, almost like reluctant concessions, crumbs from the secularists' table. What is needed is legislation that embodies and recognises these basic religious freedoms as a human right.

That sounds suspiciously like a Human Rights Act to me.

In their submission to the Commonwealth's recent inquiry into the harmonisation of discrimination legislation, Professors Patrick Parkinson and Nicholas Aroney observe:

> Great care needs to be taken to ensure that a focus on the first-mentioned right (freedom from discrimination) does not diminish the others (eg freedom of religion, association and cultural expression and practice). This can readily happen, for example, if freedom of religion is respected only grudgingly and at the margins of anti-discrimination law as a concessionary 'exception' to general prohibitions on discrimination. It can also happen if inadequate attention is paid to freedom of association and the rights of groups to celebrate and practise their faith and culture together.

These dangers are real. Some advocates for reform of anti-discrimination laws have a tendency to place a very high value on 'non-discrimination' and to concede 'exceptions' based upon freedom of religion, association or cultural expression only with great reluctance, if at all. Although they sometimes recognise that there is a need to give due weight to all human rights and to find an appropriate balance between them, it is generally not acknowledged that posing the question as one of identifying exceptions to the principle of non-discrimination prejudices the inquiry in favour of the right to be free of discrimination and against the rights to freedom of religion, association and culture, understood as both individual and group rights.

If all schools or even the majority of schools were faith-based, there would be a stronger case for anti-discrimination provisions applying more broadly in employment situations for teachers. When seeking to balance conflicting rights, there may be a case for permitting a fuller expression of religious liberty when alternatives exist elsewhere in society for persons seeking non-discriminatory opportunities or services. For example, the UK has now decided to insist that all registered adoption agencies within the jurisdiction, including Catholic ones, provide a non-discriminatory service such that adoption would be as readily available to a same sex couple as to a man and woman wanting to adopt a child into their family. In my opinion, it would be no interference with the rights or dignity of gay and lesbian couples if some religious adoption agencies acting on their religious beliefs gave preference to married heterosexual couples when determining adoptive parents for a child, provided always that the agency was acting in the best interests of the child. Provided only that there is a range of other adoption agencies providing services to all couples, including gay and lesbian couples, it is a case of legislative overreach for the State to insist on uniform non-discrimination for all agencies.

Religious vilification
Since 11 September 2001, Australians have displayed an increased sensitivity to the demands of Muslim Australians that their perspective on pressing social and political questions be heeded. There has been spirited debate in the Australian community about the need for religious vilification laws to protect Muslims from uninformed attack by Christian fundamentalists. During the 2009 National Human Rights Consultation, we heard individuals, even church leaders, expressing concern that a national charter of rights might entail a national religious vilification law similar to that in Victoria. The Victorian law (enacted before the Charter and therefore without the benefit of a statement of compatibility) provides:

> A person must not, on the ground of the religious belief or activity of another person or class of persons, engage in conduct that incites hatred against, serious contempt for, or revulsion or severe ridicule of, that other person or class of persons.

In my view, the application of the Victorian religious vilification law has hindered rather than helped religious and social harmony. The Catch the Fires litigation in Victoria has placed a permanent cloud over the utility of all religious vilification laws in Australia. These laws cannot be administered with sufficient transparency and neutrality. Even if one were to accept the utility and desirability of racial vilification laws (which incidentally I do not, and never have), there is a strong case for stopping short of religious vilification laws or for at least enacting such laws only for criminal prosecution at the behest of the Attorney General. While it is inherently racist for a person to claim membership of the best race, it is no bad thing for a religious person to claim membership of the one true religion. That is the very point of religious belief. That is what religious people do. Within the great religious traditions, there are strands which urge universal respect and love for all persons regardless of their religious affiliation. But the State overreaches itself when it simplistically replicates a racial vilification law into a religious vilification law. A racial vilification law prohibits vilification on the grounds of a physical characteristic (race) and is premised on the absolute equality of all variants of that physical characteristic (in this instance, race) and on the moral necessity for all persons to accord the same respect to persons regardless of their manifestation of that physical characteristic (race). A religious vilification law prohibits vilification on the grounds of religious belief when there is no necessary presumption by believers that all religions are equally good and true, and when central to the religious creed of some believers is the rejection of all other religious creeds. In a free and democratic society, there is a need to accommodate religious beliefs which are critical of other religious beliefs, precisely because those beliefs are different. Some fanatical, fundamentalist religious practitioners might be rightly reviled or ridiculed. Other religious practitioners might deserve to be respected regardless of the errancy of their beliefs or the potential of their beliefs to be misconstrued by others for destructive purposes. The state overreaches itself when it purports to make laws distinguishing what classes of religious critiques are warranted. The state is on safer ground when it makes laws prohibiting vilification on the grounds of race.

After the Catch the Fires litigation had been remitted to VCAT having been all the way to the Victorian Court of Appeal, the parties ultimately reached a confidential settlement on 22 June 2007—five years and three months after the offending seminar, four years and four months after the VCAT proceedings had first commenced, and with legal bills presumably run up to millions of dollars. VCAT published a fairly innocuous, self-evident agreed statement by the parties.

A welcome statement of principle about religious tolerance, it highlighted the futility of the years of litigation over religious vilification. There are no grounds for thinking that such litigation does anything to foster greater religious understanding and tolerance, nor to provide greater protection and dignity for the practitioners of minority religions. There are many Australians who still carry a sense of grievance that these two religious pastors have been subjected to the full weight of the law, having had to expend much time and resources, only to have the complainants come away with a laudable joint statement about respect and difference. Ironically, the whole nation became more appraised of the views of Messrs Scot and Naliah about Islam than they would ever have imagined possible when they first started their seminars. The formal agreed published statement at the end of the Catch the Fires proceedings is marked by nothing other than blandness and even-handedness, coming at the end of a very rancorous public debate about the core beliefs of Islam.

Sharia
There is a place for religious law in the secular courts. Carolyn Evans looks at the use of secular law in resolving intra-religious disputes, the use or enforcement of religious law in secular courts, and the establishment of formally recognised religious courts. She concludes:

> For some religious people, the opportunity to have their disputes settled by religious law with religious judges is an essential part of their culture and personal beliefs.

> For others (including some people from the same religious tradition) such an approach is a threat to the notion of equality under the law and the separation of church and state. Even when the secular legal system does not give formal recognition to religious law, it is difficult to prevent informal mechanisms to dispute resolution urging if there is sufficient demand for it in a religious community. For some, this is an argument for resisting such developments in Australia. For others, it is a warning that it is better to work with such legal systems to ensure that they comply with basic human rights and procedural fairness, rather than to keep them outside the fold where there are no such guarantees. As Australia becomes more multi-religious, these disputes are likely to become more frequent.

The recognition of universal human rights and the proper delimitation of such rights does not entail all persons being treated the same before the law of the State. Rowan Williams occasioned great controversy in his 2008 Address at the Law Courts of London entitled. 'Civil and Religious Law in England: A Religious Perspective'. Much as Pope Benedict later did at the UN, he set out the claim that universalist claims to human rights and human dignity are derived from comprehensive world views informed by religious tradition. More inclusive than Pope Benedict, he broadened his attention from Christianity to include Judaism and Islam, observing:

> It never does any harm to be reminded that without certain themes consistently and strongly emphasised by the 'Abrahamic' faiths, themes to do with the unconditional possibility for every human subject to live in conscious relation with God and in free and constructive collaboration with others, there is no guarantee that a 'universalist' account of human dignity would ever have seemed plausible or even emerged with clarity.

But then he went on to deal with the issue of British Muslims being able to invoke Sharia law:

> I have been arguing that a defence of an unqualified secular legal monopoly in terms of the need for a universalist doctrine of human right or dignity is to misunderstand the circumstances in which that doctrine emerged, and that the essential liberating (and religiously informed) vision it represents is not imperilled by a loosening of the monopolistic framework. At the moment, one of the most frequently noted problems in the law in this area is the reluctance of a dominant rights-based philosophy to acknowledge the liberty of conscientious opting-out from collaboration in procedures or practices that are in tension with the demands of particular religious groups: the assumption, in rather misleading shorthand, that if a right or liberty is granted there is a corresponding duty upon every individual to 'activate' this whenever called upon.

Williams has no difficulty conceding that citizens can boast 'multiple affiliations' within the nation State. There are instances when a citizen ought to be entitled to resolve a conflict within his own ethnic community or according to the laws and tradition of her own religion.

Five months later, Lord Phillips, now President of the Supreme Court of the UK, who had chaired the Archbishop of Canterbury's lecture, gave his own endorsement:

> It was not very radical to advocate embracing Sharia Law in the context of family disputes, for example, and our system already goes a long way towards accommodating the Archbishop's suggestion. It is possible in this country for those who are entering into a contractual agreement to agree that the agreement shall be governed by a law other than English law. Those who, in this country, are in dispute as to their respective rights are free to subject that dispute to the mediation

of a chosen person, or to agree that the dispute shall be resolved by a chosen arbitrator or arbitrators. There is no reason why principles of Sharia Law, or any other religious code should not be the basis for mediation or other forms of alternative dispute resolution. It must be recognised, however, that any sanctions for a failure to comply with the agreed terms of the mediation would be drawn from the laws of England and Wales. So far as aspects of matrimonial law are concerned, there is a limited precedent for English law to recognise aspects of religious laws, although when it comes to divorce this can only be effected in accordance with the civil law of this country.

The State can still insist on monogamy, prohibiting the contracting of more than one marriage and criminalising bigamy. That is because the State has a legitimate interest in restricting marriage such that equal dignity and respect is accorded all parties to the marriage. The State encounters a problem with the polygamist who legally registers only one marriage while living in more than one 'marriage' relationship consistent with cultural or religious norms foreign to the mainstream legal system. There are good reasons of public policy for the State refusing to lend legal weight to a religious polygamist wanting to enforce any agreement relating to any second or subsequent 'marriage' while the first marriage is still recognised by law as being the only marriage capable of legal recognition. State recognition of monogamy and criminalisation of bigamy are justified even when some citizens hold religious beliefs permitting bigamy. The civil law can properly override religious belief and practice when such belief or practice is counter to the fundamental equality of all citizens. There is however a significant grey area: when Muslims (or any other persons) decide not to have their marriages performed by an authorised celebrant and registered under the Commonwealth Marriage Act. There may be issues with a person entering into multiple de facto marriages or even of entering into a de facto marriage with a person under the lawful marriage age. These problems should be addressed by the law in the same way whether or not any of the parties are Muslim.

Religious individuals and organisations can make a good case for opting out of the State regime when there is no risk to the fundamental human rights or human dignity of any party affected by the action. There are sure to be border line cases. My father, a retired Chief Justice of Australia, when delivering the 2012 Hal Wootten Lecture at the University of New South Wales said he found Rowan Williams's view misconceived. He observed:

> Therefore a Muslim is free to adhere to the beliefs, customs and practices prescribed by Sharia law insofar as they are consistent with the general law in force in this country. That freedom must be respected and protected but that does not mean that Islamic Sharia should have the force of law.

He joined issue with a claim by the President of the Federal Supreme Court of the United Arab Emirates that the basic principles of Islamic Sharia are provided by

> [b]oth the Koran and the Sunna [which] could be considered the constitution in other legislation systems, and therefore all other sources should agree with them. Thus, if juristic reasoning contradicts with them, it should be rendered invalid, and if customs contradict with them, they are also unacceptable; and this applies to all other secondary or ancillary sources.

Putting to one side the observation about Rowan Williams' misconception and focusing on the claim by the Muslim judge, I respectfully agree with my father who asserted:

> The common law does not go so far—it leaves a gap between the mandates of the law and the conduct that we choose to engage in according to our individual moral standards. We call that gap 'freedom' and it allows Australian law to protect the cultural moral values of our minorities. We value that freedom not only for the benefit of the individual but in order to maintain a free society.

The real challenge for the future is determining the width of that gap not just for individuals but also for groups bound together by religious faith which differs from the comprehensive worldview of the Australian majority. We know the gap is real for Muslims; it may also be a widening gap for Christians and Orthodox Jews wanting to profess and live their faith individually and collectively while honouring the values which unite us as Australians governed by the rule of law.

The same sex marriage debate

The confusion over religion and politics is presently being played out in Australia over this same sex marriage debate. A while ago I wrote a lengthy letter to a bishop explaining why I disagreed with his public statements on same sex marriage and civil unions. He never even acknowledged the letter. Next time we met socially, it was a case of 'Don't mention the war.' It's clear. He's a bishop; I'm not. No correspondence will be entered into. How are we to formulate credible arguments in the square of a pluralistic democratic society when we don't even talk to each other? A month or two later, I was convinced by the secretariat of the Catholic bishops' conference to appear on television to discuss same sex marriage because none of the twelve bishops approached was available. When I got there I found that the Catholic Church was the only mainstream Christian denomination represented. That was hardly fair to the others.

Before appearing on the program, I did three things. I had asked the congregation at my regular Sunday mass for comment after mass. Many older parishioners said that they did not want to see any discrimination against same sex couples but they were not sure that a same sex relationship was the same as their marriage. I asked a young couple whose marriage I had recently performed with a nuptial mass what they thought, and they made it very clear to me that for their generation the whole discussion was a bit of a yawn and the answer for civil law was self-evident. I called a lesbian Catholic I knew who had children with her partner and she told me that she was a lesbian and always would be; that she was Catholic and always would be; that the clergy should get over this idea that they were the gatekeepers to the gospels and the sacraments because the key message was that God is love.

I am a supporter of civil unions. Conceding that neither side of the debate is much interested in that outcome, I have concluded that we can no longer draw a line between civil unions and same sex marriage. During the recent federal election, Kevin Rudd pulled out all stops to advocate same sex marriage legislation in the Commonwealth Parliament. Tony Abbott stuck firmly to the line that his party would maintain party policy that marriage is a relationship between one man and one woman to the exclusion of others, and that the party policy would be maintained unless and until the party revised its position, including whether or not to allow a conscience vote. In the Liberal Party, as distinct from the Labor Party, members are always free to cross the floor without the risk of automatic expulsion from the party—though their prospects of promotion tend to take a nosedive.

Any extension of the civil law's definition of marriage should be the preserve of the Commonwealth Parliament with all members being granted a conscience vote. Presently the 1961 Commonwealth Marriage Act as amended states that 'marriage means the union of a man and a woman to the exclusion of all others, voluntarily entered into for life'.

Under the Australian Constitution, the Commonwealth Parliament has power to make laws with respect to marriage. So too do the States. And since 1978, so too does the ACT Legislative Assembly. But if a Commonwealth law purports to cover the field, any State or Territory law does not operate to the extent of any inconsistency. Undoubtedly the Commonwealth will argue in the High Court that it has covered the field on marriage since 1961 and it should be left to do so. Advocates for 'marriage equality' frustrated by the slow pace of change at a Commonwealth level have decided to pursue state and territory legislation for forms of unequal and inferior marriage recognition in the hope of providing further political pressure for the Commonwealth to act.

Some strong advocates of traditional marriage, including the Australian Christian Lobby, have been suggesting that the matter should be resolved by referendum. That is a bad idea. In Australia, we expect our members of parliament to make the statutory law and our judges to shape the common law and interpret the Constitution. We the people vote by referendum only to change the Constitution. Occasionally there is a case to be made for a plebiscite when we are trying to determine a particular question to put to the people by referendum to change the Constitution. This is what we did when we wanted to determine whether we were ready to vote for a particular form of republic.

Groups like the Australian Christian Lobby should be careful what they wish for. If a referendum on same sex marriage, why not a referendum on (say) the death penalty? If the opinion polls are right, there is no doubt the way that one would go. Or a referendum on excluding boat people from Australia? Or a referendum on euthanasia? There are good reasons for avoiding the populist politics of lawmaking by direct popular vote of the people.

As a Catholic priest and as an Australian citizen I think the public good would be best served by all parties in the federal parliament being granted a conscience vote on same sex marriage. I oppose same sex marriage laws being enacted in state and territory parliaments because they would be either inoperative or disruptive of a national code while providing an unequal form of marriage.

I think our federal politicians voting according to conscience and not according to party dictate will be well positioned to judge when the country is ready to make the change to marriage by including the unions of same sex couples. If and when they do, I will not lose any sleep over it and I will be delighted for those same sex couples who think it will help social support and endorsement of their faithful committed relationships. I will spare a thought for those older married Australians who remain unconvinced that a same sex marriage relationship is the same as theirs. I will remain vigilant that State laws and policies should not encourage the creation of children without a known biological father and known biological mother.

The asylum and border protection debate

During the 2013 federal election, we Australians were confronted with our major political parties trying to outbid each other with a 'shock and awe' campaign aimed at 'stopping the boats'. Some of us tried to be prophetic with our denunciations. Others pragmatically tried to temper the likely callous outcomes.

In terms of the short-term solution to the loss of life at sea and the expanding trade of the people smugglers luring increasing numbers of asylum seekers to Indonesia for transit to Australia, we all need to work within the reality that all major political parties in Australia are committed to a shock and awe approach. Some of us are prepared to discuss how that shock and awe approach might be tailored to be less callous and objectionable. Others find it so objectionable as to not warrant discussion. Many of us are just deeply troubled and have no idea what to do or say, hoping the problem will go away soon. If in the midst of the evil of the present situation, I can do something to save one life or to accord proper protection to one additional refugee I will do it. I am very grateful that people schooled in Christian social teaching have been prepared to engage in ongoing dialogue on this issue.

When confronted with moral evil in public policy, church personnel always have a choice: to be prophetic, sticking to the moral absolutes (like the Greens or the US-style Right to Life Movement), or to be practical, engaging in the compromises needed to temper the evil (like the major political parties and those who agitate for better welfare measures for mothers so that they might be less likely to choose abortion). Whichever option we take, we all need to concede that at the moment, the only political parties not wanting to embrace a short term shock and awe approach are the Greens, the DLP and the Palmer United Party. I wish them all the best, but neither Christine Milne, John Madigan nor Clive Palmer will ever be prime minister.

Words, actions and structures all have their part to play. During the 2013 election, the boys at St Ignatius College Riverview of their own accord wrote to Tony Abbott and all the other Jesuit alumni in the major political parties:

> We feel compelled to express our disappointment that, as graduates of our Jesuit schools, you would allow those principles, cultivated in our common tradition, to be betrayed. We look for heroes among our alumni, for *insignes* (generous and influential people, as Ignatius styled them). Instead we see only allegiances to parties that trade human lives for political expediency, that choose the lowest common denominator to woo the populace, and that speak of economic problems rather than the dignity of the human person, especially the most vulnerable.

This was highly prophetic language.

Riverview is a very different school from what it was in Tony Abbott's day. One structural difference is that there are now routine scholarships for indigenous Australians and for refugees. So the life experience of the boys is different. Their reflection on their school experience is different. It was this difference that helped to motivate the boys of 2013 to write. The chief author of the letter told the media that the boys had been listening to the stories of their refugee mates:

> Knowing first-hand the direct conflicts they have faced and seeing politicians making decisions that aren't taking into account humanity made us very upset. We wanted to evoke the feeling of what they experienced at Riverview and try to remind them that, when it comes right down to it, it's not about making decisions based on politics. It's about trying to come back to core values.

Tony Abbott has been receiving a number of letters from students educated in Christian social teaching. Isabel Teixeira, a Year 12 student at Good Counsel College, Innisfail, daughter of a Timorese refugee, wrote him a five-page letter saying,

> If this proposed policy or even the current policy had been established and implemented when my father was seeking asylum from the war in Timor-Leste in the 1970s, I would not exist. However, they were not the policies of the 1970s and, as a result, my father was able to live in Australia, work as a member of parliament in both Australia and Timor-Leste, owns his own law firm and has educated his own children to understand the importance of human rights conservation. Is this not a gain for Australia? Mr Abbott, you know the facts, and if having them reiterated has still not evoked some form of recognition of the illegality of the policies, then I would like you to consider this: by you turning back these boats, carrying people who are potentially escaping situations which most Australians would consider

nothing less than horrific, you are turning your back on any inkling of humanity which, through your actions, Australia maintains.

These prophetic utterances from young Catholics will not win the day on their own. But they are not useless. They are not simply romantic doodlings of out-of-touch do-gooders. Pope Francis has been very prophetic in his utterances on the same topic. The island Lampedusa is the European equivalent of our hellish Christmas Island. It is a lightning rod for European concerns about the security of borders in an increasingly globalised world where people as well as capital flow across porous borders. That's why Pope Francis went there on his first official papal visit outside Rome. At Lampedusa on 8 July 2013, Pope Francis said:

> 'Where is your brother?' Who is responsible for this blood? In Spanish literature we have a comedy of Lope de Vega which tells how the people of the town of Fuente Ovejuna kill their governor because he is a tyrant. They do it in such a way that no one knows who the actual killer is. So when the royal judge asks: 'Who killed the governor?', they all reply: 'Fuente Ovejuna, sir'. Everybody and nobody! Today too, the question has to be asked: Who is responsible for the blood of these brothers and sisters of ours? Nobody! That is our answer: It isn't me; I don't have anything to do with it; it must be someone else, but certainly not me. Yet God is asking each of us: 'Where is the blood of your brother which cries out to me?' Today no one in our world feels responsible; we have lost a sense of responsibility for our brothers and sisters. We have fallen into the hypocrisy of the priest and the Levite whom Jesus described in the parable of the Good Samaritan: we see our brother half dead on the side of the road, and perhaps we say to ourselves: 'poor soul . . . !', and then go on our way. It's not our responsibility, and with that we feel reassured, assuaged. The culture of comfort, which makes us think only of ourselves, makes us insensitive to the cries

of other people, makes us live in soap bubbles which, however lovely, are insubstantial; they offer a fleeting and empty illusion which results in indifference to others; indeed, it even leads to the globalisation of indifference. In this globalised world, we have fallen into globalised indifference. We have become used to the suffering of others: it doesn't affect me; it doesn't concern me; it's none of my business!

Here we can think of Manzoni's character—'the Unnamed'. The globalisation of indifference makes us all 'unnamed', responsible, yet nameless and faceless.

Then on his recent visit to the Jesuit Church in Rome Pope Francis said:

After Lampedusa and other places of arrival, our city, Rome, is the second stage for many people. Often—as we heard—it's a difficult, exhausting journey; what you face can even be violent—I'm thinking above all of the women, of mothers, who endure this to ensure a future for their children and the hope of a different life for themselves and their family. Rome should be the city that allows refugees to rediscover their humanity, to start smiling again. Instead, too often, here, as in other places, so many people who carry residence permits with the words 'international protection' on them are constrained to live in difficult, sometimes degrading, situations, without the possibility of building a life in dignity, of thinking of a new future!

Those of us schooled in the Christian tradition often contemplate the parable of the Good Samaritan, as Pope Francis did when at Lampedusa. That parable works well for one stray Jew fallen by the wayside in desperate need. It works even better when the travelling Samaritan has access to a trusting Jewish innkeeper who will offer credit on spec. It needs some imaginative discernment once you postulate hundreds fallen by the wayside, millions even more desperate in faraway places, and institutional innkeepers who have shareholders or voters to satisfy. The gospel message of charity and justice must always be prophetic, pedagogical and practical. The democratically elected leaders of a robust pluralist nation such as Australia have to accept that they cannot help everyone in need on the planet and they are elected to maintain secure borders and a standard of living for our citizens which could not be emulated for all persons on the planet.

Though most of our neighbours are not signatories to the Refugee Convention, Australia should remain a party to the Convention, and refugee advocates should stop overstating or mis-stating the rights protected by the Convention and the UN Declaration of Human Rights (UNDHR). Article 14(1) of the UNDHR provides: 'Everyone has the right to seek and to enjoy in other countries asylum from persecution.' Back in 1948, the drafters had suggested that a person have the right to be 'granted asylum'—a legal right to just turn up here by boat! Australia was one of the strong, successful opponents, being prepared to acknowledge only the individual's right 'to seek and enjoy asylum', because such a right would not include the right to enter another country and it would not create a duty for a country to permit entry by the asylum seeker. That's why Article 31(1) of the Refugee Convention deals as it does with the illegal entry or presence of an asylum seeker who has entered or is present without authorisation. It provides:

> The Contracting States shall not impose penalties, on account of their illegal entry or presence, on refugees who, coming directly from a territory where their life or freedom was threatened in the sense of article 1, enter or are present in their territory without authorisation, provided they present themselves without delay to the authorities and show good cause for their illegal entry or presence.

The immunity from penalty is restricted to refugees 'coming directly from a territory where their life or freedom was threatened'. The Australian government website is correct when it states:

> International law recognises that people at risk of persecution have a legal right to flee their country and

> seek refuge elsewhere, but does not give them a right to enter a country of which they are not a national. Nor do people at risk of persecution have a right to choose their preferred country of protection.

There is a right to leave your country. There is a right to re-enter your country. There is a right to seek asylum. But there is no right to enter another country of which you are not a national—even to seek asylum. Should you have succeeded in entering another country not your own, whether legally or illegally, you have a right to enjoy asylum if you are a refugee.

The moral argument is another matter. But it is important to be clear about Australia's international obligations under the UNDHR and the Convention on Refugees. Unfortunately even the website of the Refugee Council of Australia is wrong when it states:

> The UN Refugee Convention (to which Australia is a signatory) recognises that refugees have a right to enter a country for the purposes of seeking asylum, regardless of how they arrive or whether they hold valid travel or identity documents.

Given that most of our neighbours are not signatories to the Refugee Convention, there is no point in over-stating our legal obligations when we come to the moral arguments and the diplomatic negotiations that will be required to enhance the processing and protection of refugees in our region. It would be folly to abandon the international legal instruments and just rely on moral argument and diplomatic negotiations. We should maintain the safety net of law. The political atmosphere is such that the safety net will become so frayed as to be useless if refugee advocates continue to overstate and mis-state the law.

There is no doubt that the reforms of July 2008 instituted by the Rudd Government and not opposed by the Nelson Opposition contributed to a sharp increase in the arrival of boat people. The annual arrivals continued to spiral upwards—from 2856, to 6689, a brief drop to 4730, then up to 17,271, and then up again to 25,145. By the time Kevin Rudd had become prime minister for the second time in June 2013 the boat arrivals were running at 3,300 per month (40,000 per annum). There was intelligence available that the people smuggling networks were now so adept at plying their trade in Indonesia that the numbers could escalate even further. These increases were not related to increased global refugee flows nor to new refugee-producing situations in the region. There had been at least 900 deaths at sea since the 2008 reforms were instituted. Something had to be done—not just for crass political gain but for sound ethical reasons.

Since the High Court's rejection of the Gillard government's Malaysia solution, there has been a need to consider how ethically and practically to stop the boats. The lack of bipartisan agreement meant that the recommendations of the Houston panel could be only partially implemented. In the medium term, it might be possible to negotiate a regional agreement involving at least Australia, Indonesia and Malaysia. An agreement, with UNHCR backing, could provide basic protection and processing for asylum seekers transiting Malaysia and Indonesia. Asylum seekers headed for Australia could then be intercepted and promptly screened to determine that none was in direct flight from persecution in Indonesia. They could then be flown back safely to Indonesia and placed at the end of a real queue. Provided the necessary screening was done, it could then be appropriate to adopt Alexander Downer's suggestion: 'Australia would fly back to Indonesia anyone who arrived here by boat without a visa. In exchange, Australia would take, one for one, UNHCR approved refugees from refugee camps in Indonesia.' Such an agreement would take many months, if not years, to negotiate and implement. Admittedly, it would not provide a short-term solution to stopping the boats.

Kevin Rudd's pre-election agreements negotiated with Papua New Guinea and Nauru and first announced on 19 July 2013 were aimed at stopping the boats. It was the equivalent of a 'shock and awe' measure, threatening dreadful outcomes for people, hopefully deterring them from even considering getting on board a boat. During the election campaign, both major political parties tried to convince the electors that they would be able to design policies which stopped the boats.

During its last year in office, Labor had increased the humanitarian component of our migration program from 13,750 to 20,000 places—with 12,000 of those places being allocated to refugees offshore, 8,000 being available for refugees onshore and the special humanitarian program. The Coalition initially supported the increase but reversed this commitment during the election campaign. The Abbott government says it will provide only 2,750 places for onshore applicants.

If adopting the key planks of the Rudd plan, the Abbott government could give the 'shock and awe' response greater ethical coherence if they took the following seven steps:

1. Tony Abbott should continue discussions with Jakarta with an eye to a negotiated agreement with both Indonesia and Malaysia aimed at upstream improvement of processing and protection.

2. The Abbott government should return to its previous commitment to increase the humanitarian quota to 20,000.

3. Scott Morrison should order an ethical reassessment of the plight of those who came by boat to Australia after the Rudd announcement of 19 July 2013 without notice of the new shock and awe policy, bearing in mind that many of those who arrived immediately after 19 July had received no notice of the new policy. This was admitted by Minister Tony Burke when he told the media on 22 August 2013: 'First week after the announcement, the figures remained very high, but let's not forget those figures include people who are already at sea.'

4. Scott Morrison should undertake to care for unaccompanied minors who arrive in Australia's territorial waters until they can be safely resettled or safely returned to their family or to the guardians in transit from whom they were separated.

5. Scott Morrison should institute safeguards, including a transparent complaints mechanism, in PNG and Nauru consistent with the safeguards recommended by the Houston Panel for both Pacific processing countries and for Malaysia under the Malaysia Solution.

6. Tony Abbott should introduce a bill to Parliament detailing the measures aimed at stopping the boats, thereby putting beyond legal doubt the 'shock and awe measures' implemented on the eve of the election campaign without parliamentary scrutiny, and locking in the major political parties so that petty party point-scoring might cease. The debate on the bill will allow both sides of the Chamber to purge themselves of the hypocrisy that has accompanied Labor's unctuous condemnation of John Howard's Pacific Solution and the Coalition's unctuous condemnation of Julia Gillard's Malaysia

Solution. The bill would undoubtedly win the support of the major political parties, restoring a more bipartisan approach as existed in July 2008 when Minister Chris Evans announced 'the seven key immigration values' then unanimously embraced by the Parliament's Joint Standing Committee on Migration.

7. The government should commit itself to the prompt processing onshore of Papuan asylum seekers in direct flight from West Papua. The Coalition's policy on asylum seekers published during the election campaign states, 'The Coalition will work with our regional partners to address the secondary movement of asylum seekers into our region as a transit point to illegally enter Australia through the establishment of a comprehensive Regional Deterrence Framework.' Papuans fleeing persecution at home are not engaged in secondary movement. If refugees, they are in direct flight from persecution. The Abbott government should recommit to our obligation under the Refugee Convention to grant asylum to refugees who have entered Australia in direct flight from persecution.

While waiting to see if the boats do stop, all Australians can consider how better to contribute to protection and processing of asylum seekers in the region.

The tools of Christian social teaching

The language of Christian social teaching must always be prophetic, pedagogical and practical. Our social teaching is not just words. It's reflected in words, actions and structures. One of the credibility problems for my Church today is that we proclaim a message of justice, inclusion, and non-discrimination within a structure which is sexist and without sufficient theological coherence or scriptural warrant, and which has been grossly neglectful of the best interests of the most vulnerable—abused children. Christian social teaching provides us with ideas, feeds our imaginations, fires our passions, underpins our conversations, and animates our celebrations in relation to faith and justice—belief in a loving God and solidarity with our fellow human beings. Being Christian, we respond as community, not as atomised individuals. Our responses are marked by service and ritual, informed by tradition and authority, as well as reflection on lived experience.

The last three popes have armed us Catholics with some wonderful concepts for taking on the task of shaping a world bearing more the marks of the Kingdom to come.

In his 1988 encyclical *Sollicitudo Rei Socialis*, Pope John II spoke of the interdependence of the head and the solidarity of the heart.

> However much society worldwide shows signs of fragmentation, expressed in the conventional names First, Second, Third and even Fourth World, their interdependence remains close. When this interdependence is separated from its ethical requirements, it has disastrous consequences for the weakest. Indeed, as a result of a sort of internal dynamic and under the impulse of mechanisms which can only be called perverse, this interdependence triggers negative effects even in the rich countries. It is precisely within these countries that one encounters, though on a lesser scale, the more specific manifestations of underdevelopment. Thus it should be obvious that development either becomes shared in common by every part of the world or it undergoes a process of regression even in zones marked by constant progress. This tells us a great deal about the nature of authentic development: either all the nations of the world participate, or it will not be true development.

Inviting us to move from the head to the heart, from thinking to taking a stand, Pope John Paul II then spoke of solidarity:

> At the same time, in a world divided and beset by every type of conflict, the conviction is growing of a radical interdependence and consequently of the need for a solidarity which will take up interdependence and transfer it to the moral plane. Today perhaps more than in the past, people are realising that they are linked together by a common destiny, which is to be constructed together, if catastrophe for all is to be avoided. From the depth of anguish and fear . . . , the idea is slowly emerging that the good to which we are all called and the happiness to which we aspire cannot be

obtained without an effort and commitment on the part of all, nobody excluded, and the consequent renouncing of personal selfishness.

Pope Benedict XVI gave us useful insights into the relationship between faith and politics in his encyclical *Deus Caritas Est*:

> Justice is both the aim and the intrinsic criterion of all politics. Politics is more than a mere mechanism for defining the rules of public life: its origin and its goal are found in justice, which by its very nature has to do with ethics. The State must inevitably face the question of how justice can be achieved here and now. But this presupposes an even more radical question: what is justice? The problem is one of practical reason; but if reason is to be exercised properly, it must undergo constant purification, since it can never be completely free of the danger of a certain ethical blindness caused by the dazzling effect of power and special interests.

Here politics and faith meet. Faith by its specific nature is an encounter with the living God—an encounter opening up new horizons extending beyond the sphere of reason. But it is also a purifying force for reason itself. From God's standpoint, faith liberates reason from its blind spots and therefore helps it to be ever more fully itself. Faith enables reason to do its work more effectively and to see its proper object more clearly. This is where Catholic social doctrine has its place: it has no intention of giving the Church power over the State. Even less is it an attempt to impose on those who do not share the faith ways of thinking and modes of conduct proper to faith. Its aim is simply to help purify reason and to contribute, here and now, to the acknowledgment and attainment of what is just.

Pope Francis, anxious to demonstrate the continuity of our social teaching, made few changes to Benedict's draft of what was to be his last encyclical and published *Lumen Fidei* in 2013 as his own first encyclical. Francis speaks of the contemporary relevance of our faith for all people, helping us to contribute to the common good:

> Faith is truly a good for everyone; it is a common good. Its light does not simply brighten the interior of the Church, nor does it serve solely to build an eternal city in the hereafter; it helps us build our societies in such a way that they can journey towards hope.

These concepts of interdependence and solidarity, the relationship between faith and politics, and the assurance that Christian faith can assist everyone committed to justice and the common good can be harnessed prophetically, pedagogically, and practically to formulate our proposals, actions and structures for a more just and peaceful world. They are the building blocks which come to life when we wrestle with a question such as how we might make our asylum policy more humane and more just.

Prophetic remarks need to be matched by practical suggestions. We need to come to the table of practical deliberation committed to finding a better way to treat those who risk all on boats so that they might live. By forming and informing ourselves in Christian social teaching we can contribute to a more just world prophetically, pedagogically and practically. Within the church community we can sponsor the respectful dialogue needed so that the inevitable compromises of politics can be better tailored to justice for us all—acknowledging our interdependence and standing firm in solidarity. In the contemporary public square, much of the dialogue will be conducted using the language of human rights.

Once we investigate much of the contemporary discussion about human rights, we find that often the intended recipients of rights do not include all human beings but only those with certain capacities or those who share sufficient common attributes with the decision makers. It is always at the edges that there is real work for human rights discourse to do. It is not surprising that religious persons often have a keen eye for the neediest, not only espousing their rights but taking action for their wellbeing and human flourishing. Speaking at the London School of Economics on 'Religious Faith and Human Rights', Rowan Williams, the Archbishop of Canterbury, boldly and correctly asserted:

> The question of foundations for the discourse of non-negotiable rights is not one that lends itself to simple resolution in secular terms; so it is not at all odd if diverse ways of framing this question in religious terms flourish so persistently. The uncomfortable truth is that a purely secular account of human rights is always going to be problematic if it attempts to establish a language of rights as a supreme and non-contestable governing concept in ethics.

No one should pretend that the discourse about universal ethics and inalienable rights has a firmer foundation than it actually has. Williams concluded his lecture with this observation:

> As in other areas of political or social thinking, theology is one of those elements that continues to pose questions about the legitimacy of what is said and what is done in society, about the foundations of law itself. The secularist way may not have an answer and may not be convinced that the religious believer has an answer that can be generally accepted; but our discussion of social and political ethics will be a great deal poorer if we cannot acknowledge the force of the question.

Once we abandon any religious sense that the human person is created in the image and likeness of God and that God has commissioned even the powerful to act justly, love tenderly and walk humbly with their God, it may be very difficult to maintain a human rights commitment to the weakest and most despised in society. It may come down to the vote, moral sentiment, tribal affiliations, or the national interest. And that will not be enough to extend human rights universally. In the name of utility, the society spared religious influence will have one less impediment to limiting social inclusion to those like us, 'us' being the decision makers who determine which common characteristics render embodied persons eligible for human rights protection. Nicholas Wolterstorff says, 'Our moral subculture of rights is as frail as it is remarkable. If the secularisation thesis proves true, we must expect that that subculture will have been a brief shining episode in the odyssey of human beings on earth.'

Religion does not provide the answers to difficult questions about law, politics and economics. But religious faith and religious traditions can help key actors to purify their motives and their thinking as they wrestle with concepts and strategies posited on truth and justice. Religious faith can help the believer accord respect and dignity to all persons as he or she is involved in the complexities of the market, the State and civil society. Animated by faith, hope and love, sustained and nourished by our religious traditions, we as the community of believers can engage positively in helping promote human wellbeing in Australia and beyond. Our key challenges are to be credible, relevant, and distinctive, aligning our resources, structures, actions and utterances. We need to be prophetic, pedagogical and practical. Our key responsibilities are: being a leaven in the public square fostering hope and love; enabling the forming and informing of consciences; being able respectfully to eyeball decision makers and those impacted adversely by their decisions; advocating and acting for freedom of religion, the rights of the poor and marginalised, the common good, and the stewardship of creation for future generations.

Our task is simple: out of our religious traditions we are able to stand in solidarity with all those affected adversely by prospective laws and policies; we are able disinterestedly to acknowledge the complexities of interdependence—holding in tension individual rights and entitlements together with the common good and the public interest; we participate in the public conversation respectfully with all those willing to engage, and not just with our co-religionists, 'simply to help purify reason and to contribute, here and now, to the acknowledgment and attainment of what is just'.

Forum for Theology in the World Vol 1 No 2/2014

The Salvation Army and Social Commitment

Major Jenny Begent

Introduction:

The topic 'Key Challenges and Responsibilities of the Churches in the Current Social and Cultural Context' is a topic not restricted to the twenty-first century. Since its beginnings, the church has had to grapple with its place in the society in which it lives (or in some cases, exists alongside of). Reinhold Niebuhr says a brief glance at the Gospels tells us that neither Jesus nor his disciples found an easy answer. In the person of Jesus we see a man with great love and great concern for the lost and the society in which he lived, yet paradoxically a man with a staggering lack of interest in conserving the institutions and culture of that society.[1] The post-modern church of today is, like the early church, confronted with the evidence of misery in the life of our communities, and all too often, weakness within itself.

You and I live today in a world that has abject physical poverty, religious war, economic abuse by the powerful and a profound spiritual confusion that means decision-making at the highest level is often made hesitantly, uncertainly and with a measure of self-interest. As Christ wept over Jerusalem, we may well weep over our own post-modern society in which—dare I say it—we, as the church, have often colluded to maintain the status quo.

The Salvation Army is a relative newcomer to the history of the church, having only been present since the 1860s so not yet 200 years

---

1. H Richard Niebuhr, 'The Responsibility of the Church for Society', Chapter 5, in *The Gospel, the World and the Church,* edited by Kenneth Scott Latourette (New York: Harper and Brothers, 1946). As Sterling Professor of Christian Ethics at Yale University Divinity School, Niebuhr was a very eminent scholar and writer. http://www.religion-online.org/showarticle.asp?title=2731

old. In a relatively short space of time in human history, 150 years, we have spread to be present in 117 countries, and have the distinction of being in the top five most recognised brands in the world. The question for us today is: did we do something right? Or did we do something wrong? I suspect only history will provide the answer.

The first of the Salvation Army articles of faith describes Scripture as foundational to both Christian belief and Christian living: 'We believe that the Scriptures of the Old and New Testaments were given by inspiration of God, and that they only constitute the Divine rule of Christian faith and practice.'[2] Any conversation regarding The Salvation Army's commitment to an active role in society must begin with understanding the Scripture in relation to the personal and corporate responses required by God's people.

God reveals himself through Scripture, so he establishes justice, demonstrated by love and mercy, as a foundational element of God's character. Through Jesus the kingdom of God comes into being, redemption is offered which affects the whole of creation. As a result, those who follow Christ are commissioned to work to fulfil the kingdom, a kingdom that has at its centre justice, tempered by love and mercy. So the followers of Jesus are commissioned to work toward the fulfilment of the kingdom, with justice as the central reference point, and for the church, including the Salvation Army, justice becomes not only social justice but kingdom justice.[3]

The Salvation Army has strong traditions that have shaped our understanding and theology; two are particularly relevant to our topic–a call to the marginalised, and a culture of activism. The Salvation Army's beginnings can be found in the poverty-stricken East End of London during the Victorian era. This, combined with the Booths' (Catherine Booth in particular) strong social awareness, has ensured a strong historical commitment to the poor and marginalised which continues to the present day. The Salvation Army has always been a 'neighbourhood religion,'[4] growing as society has grown and

---

2. See *Salvation Story, Salvationist Handbook of Doctrine* (London: Salvation Army International Headquarters, 1998), 1–12. http://salvationist.ca/wp-content/uploads/2009/02/sastory.pdf
3. Lieut Col Karen Shakespeare, 'Fulfilling the Great Commission in the 21st Century: Outworking of the Response—Social Justice. The Salvation Army and Social Justice', paper delivered to International Doctrine Council of the Salvation Army, February 2009, http://www.salvationarmt.org/isjc/tsasocialjustice
4. Shakespeare, 'Fulfilling the Great Commission'.

led by the local community. The founders, William and Catherine Booth, were profoundly influenced by the theology of John Wesley, for whom 'social righteousness' was essential to the holy life.

However, although he is known to have welcomed the very poor into his local Methodist church as a youth, much to the annoyance of the congregation, history records that it is not until 1888, returning home late at night and seeing the homeless men sleeping under the London bridges, that Booth truly recognised the need for The Salvation Army to act. This led to Booth's 1890 work, Darkest England and the Way Out, which outlined comprehensive plans to combat a wide variety of social ills of the time, and consequently gave the Salvation Army renewed focus.

We would claim to be a prophetic tradition in both theology and practice. In our early days we stood outside the circles of social and political influence. We utilised models and programs that appealed to an unsophisticated poor, who were often viewed by the mainstream church as crude and of little or no consequence. Fortunately the opinion of the established church didn't stop those early Salvationists who realised the value of a visible, lived faith with a mission focus. This response has underpinned the development of the organisation and its response to the society in which it exists. John Coutts writes: 'It would seem that the Army is at its best when confronted by a tangible social evil that it can get its teeth into.'[5] The pursuit of social justice became a feature of the Army's response to societal need and as a result, many instances in our history illustrate how the pressure applied by the Salvation Army brought about significant social and legislative changes.

However, it is to be acknowledged that the Salvation Army has in the twenty-first century become what it walked out of, part of the established church. In Australia, we are older than Federation and an integral part of the Australian fabric. Our claim of political neutrality has provided us with the excuse to engage in active social service rather than speak prophetically against the causes of injustice. With vast numbers of social service programmes throughout the world, we have, in some countries been thought of as a social service agency rather than as a church whose involvement in social issues is an act of charity in the best sense. This is certainly true in Australia, where in Melbourne we operate the largest social service response

---

5. John Coutts, *The Salvationists* (London: Mowbrays, 1977), 85

in the Salvation Army worldwide. Nevertheless, as we have worked, the dignity and self-worth of individuals were restored and renewed, and the commands of Jesus obeyed as the hungry have been fed and the prisoner visited. Despite this, there are the voices of many who would say we have sold our birthright for reputation and position. Geoff Ryan, a leading Salvationist writer, has said: 'If any blessing has departed from the Army, it is more likely over this abdication of our prophetic role than over anything else. In our youth, we innovated and customised. In our old age, we imitate and franchise'.[6]

Lt Col Karen Shakespeare expresses it thus:

> The history of The Salvation Army also records our failure to truly seek justice, to remain silent rather than have a voice that is loud enough to be heard. This failure to speak is often stated as allowing us to have freedom in ministry and the opportunity to offer help to some of those most severely affected by a lack of justice in social and government policy.[7]

In contemporary Australia this is seen in our work with asylum seekers on Manus Island and Nauru, coupled with a choice to remain silent when, in my humble opinion, we should be speaking. In this instance, the pursuit of justice for the future may jeopardise the possibility of acts of mercy in the present. It appears that to speak out is more costly than to keep silent.

From the late 1960s, one can see that the Salvation Army has slowly begun to lose its ability to hold in congruence the dual components of evangelism and social justice. William Booth once described them as 'Siamese twins—to kill one is to slay both'. Major Phillip Needham described it as a 'two arms, one task—Evangelism and Social Service for the redemption of human life'.

> The first paradigm for social service is a person hard at work on an important task. Both of his arms are

---

6. Geoff Ryan, *Sowing Dragons: Essays in Neo-Salvationism* (The Salvation Army Canada and Bermuda, 2001), 37.
7. Shakespeare, 'Fulfilling the Great Commission'.

> fully involved in getting the job done. The goal is the redemption of fallen man, and it will require that both arms work together in co-ordination. Acceptance of this paradigm means that there can be no true Christian social service without evangelism. There must be a real marriage of the two with the larger purpose being to proclaim the Kingdom of God in the world and to help people enter it.[8]

And here lies our dilemma! How does the Salvation Army hold both those arms together whilst facing the challenge to be Christ in a constantly evolving, rapidly changing, diverse and pluralistic society?

Firstly, it is important that we 'render unto Caesar that which is Caesar's'. What I mean by that is we must participate and work within the social structures of the day. Social structures serve a purpose; they are often as helpful and supportive of individuals as they are negative. To participate within them gives the ability to be critical, realistic and prophetic. Social responsibility requires wisdom and courage in order that we speak when we need to.

Secondly, the commandment to love gives us the opportunity to be a reconciling and healing presence, ministering to society with compassion and imagination. Part of our missional mandate should always be to find new and innovative ways to address emerging issues whilst advocating for a just and peaceful resolution that serves the common good.

Thirdly, the church has an obligation to be a prophetic voice and a presence challenging social structures when it is clear they seek only to ensure the poor and marginalised remain without power. Perhaps my favourite words of Catherine Booth are these: 'There is no improving the future without disturbing the present.'[9]

So what are key challenges for the Church and more particularly for the Salvation Army in the twenty-first century? For me they are: Inclusion, Indigenous Australians, Poverty, Racism and the Same-Sex Marriage Debate.

---

8. Phillip Needham, *Community in Mission: a Salvationist Ecclesiology* (London: Salvation Army International Headquarters, 1987).
9. Catherine Booth, *Papers on Aggressive Christianity*: Chapter 3, 'Adaptation of Measures' (1880), http://www.gospeltruth.net/booth/cath_booth/agressive_christianity/cbooth_3_adaptation.htm

Inclusion

For me the overarching challenge, within which all other challenges can be viewed, is 'Inclusion'. I grew up in Launceston, Tasmania. It was a very white, Anglo Saxon, predominantly Protestant place to live. We enjoyed the odd Chinese takeaway, and the local fish shop was run by a Greek family. There were no full-blood Indigenous Australians, as they had been wiped out in almost their entirety within 30 years of settlement. Diverse it was not. Yet less than 30 years later, Launceston is a city teeming with a myriad of different races and cultures. Learning to live in and appreciate as well as enjoy the diversity of this culture has been a difficult transition for some, not least the church. For the church it should be easy, for central to the biblical message is the belief that every human being is created in the image of God and that through Christ all of society is acceptable before God. Therefore the exclusion of anyone on the basis of gender, race, colour, nationality, class, language, religion, political opinion or any other basis offends against the image of God in that person.

Because diversity is often difficult to deal with, inclusiveness does not come naturally to us. Societal, cultural and historical factors often impede our capacity to accept and tolerate. However, exclusion and isolation—the alternatives to acceptance and tolerance—are clearly not Christ-like responses to human diversity. And so it is my belief that, as we grapple with the challenges of the twenty-first century, the way the church practises inclusion will be the key to its future when we consider those issues that press in upon us in the present day.

Indigenous Australians

Despite this, exclusion and isolation have all too frequently marked our dealings with each other both in the past and present. A quick scan of the Salvation Army's membership here in Melbourne told us that many of our members had left their homes due to persecution in their own country, only to find that same persecution is alive and well in the place on which they pinned their hopes and dreams.

Our immigrant society, of which you and I are members, was established at the expense of the Indigenous peoples. The relationship between both remains a key challenge for the church, particularly as indigenous peoples are largely absent from our worshipping congregations. The mainstream churches participated in the care and education of Indigenous Australian over many years, not always in culturally sensitive ways, and while I am sure that care was given with the best intentions, we all know where the road of good intentions leads.

It is appalling to consider that Indigenous peoples are, more than 200 years later, still struggling for recognition and rights. The church has unfinished business when it comes to indigenous peoples. We have been too silent and too acquiescent–particularly as one considers the enormous gap in health, education and living standards, which alone constitutes a more than sufficient indictment. The challenge for the church is how we advocate for attitudinal change at the level of government and within society to ensure that it is understood that Indigenous Australians have the capacity and responsibility to be self-determining and self-reliant.

Poverty

Poverty has been a key challenge for the church since its beginning, and will continue to be a source of division and despair in the world. Poverty persists in our societies as the result of discrimination and exclusion, and of economic deprivation. The poor are excluded because they are poor, and this exclusion perpetuates and institutionalises their poverty. Economic globalisation was once seen to have the potential to lift people out of poverty, yet the outcomes of trade and financial liberalisation in many parts of the world have been deeply ambiguous when judged according to standards of justice and ethics. Today, the global market is ever more clearly seen as an engine for the creation of even greater wealth for the wealthy, and a closed door to the poor and 'un-competitive'. Instead, economic globalisation has been the catalyst of a fast-growing chasm between the rich and the poor. Those who have been excluded by this process—the unemployed, the homeless, and the destitute—are increasingly visible even here in Melbourne, 'the most liveable city in the world', and of course in all our affluent first-world countries. The challenge for the church is to find ways that are just, to respond to economic globalisation. Economics is a place where the church is largely absent. When we pray the Lord's prayer we pray it in community, to our Father, and ask for our daily bread. So how do we as a church act in the world in a way that means all receive their daily bread in a fair and equitable distribution of resources?

Racism, asylum seekers and refugees

One of the most ancient and persistent forms of exclusion is that based on race. Racism is a powerful and persistent undercurrent in all human societies. It never ceases to amaze me how many different and new ways we can come up with to exclude and terrorise due to a person's race. The terrorist attacks and atrocities perpetrated by certain Arab Muslim groups and individuals have encouraged prejudice against all Arabs (as well as feeding anti-Muslim sentiment). The most objectionable actions of the government of Israel in the occupied Palestinian territories have given increased credibility to anti-Semites. The undoubted difficulties of fulfilling international commitments with regard to refugees and asylum-seekers have served as rationalisations for policies that are, quite frankly, racist. It is a vexed and very complex issue, muddled by incorrect information and political manoeuvering. As a Christian people, we are called to provide care and comfort to people who come to this country seeking refuge. We now see firmly entrenched in our political system an approach that seeks to circumvent the spirit of hospitality and compassion codified in international treaties and obligations. To quote Revd Elenie Poulos of UnitingCare, 'we can now say for certain that we have lost our moral compass when it comes to compassion for asylum seekers and refugees.'[10] This response, from a country for which ninety-nine per cent of its population come from somewhere else, beggars belief. The negative, distorted and myopic political debate on refugee and asylum seeker policy has been allowed to go on for far too long. It is time for a new approach which focuses on protection rather than punishment, on facts rather than fear-mongering, and on long-term solutions rather than short-term political gain. This is the area in which the church can and must have a voice. Its mandate to be Christ in the world, himself a refugee, means that we cannot be silent.

The same-sex marriage debate

I have debated with myself as to whether to include this topic as an issue for the church. To be honest, I'm not entirely convinced that it

---

10. Revd Elenie Poulos, Director of Uniting Justice, Uniting Church Assembly, Melbourne, Press release, 19 July, 2013, at http://assembly.uca.org.au/news/item/1419-gross-failure-of-compassion-on-asylum-seekers

is. It occupies a lot of print and air space in our news streams, with almost everybody having an opinion. Salvationists themselves seem to be obsessed with it, as it occupies a lot of social media content. I suspect that for older Australians it has much more interest than for young Australians. The younger Salvationists I know can't understand the furore, for them it's a no-brainer, a demonstration of equality under the law, which in its present form is seen to be discriminatory. For the Salvation Army it is an area that causes quite deep division. No doubt like most churches, there is a wide variety of views and perspectives, for all of which a sound scriptural basis is provided. Unfortunately for the Salvation Army we recently created a media storm of our own making over the issue, which further cemented the divide between those who agree and those who don't. Like all families, though, we choose quite often not to talk about those things that stare us in the face. It is for this organisation, I think, one of the elephants in the room that we all hope will quietly go away. It does have for me a sense of the inevitable about it, almost like the twenty-first century version of the vote for women. It seems to me that it can and should be a civil matter; it is possible that the church and the state can have different positions on this issue. I also believe that this change should legally exempt religious institutions from any requirement to change their historic position and practice that marriage is exclusively between a man and a woman. I agree with Fr Frank Brennan—let it be a conscience vote rather than a political vote.

Conclusion

The way we as a Christian church, in Australia today, respond to each other internally and externally, and to other religions, in a way that is inclusive and accepting, is crucial to our ongoing participation and management within society. The rise of fundamentalism and extremism is evident in elements of many of the world's major religions, Christianity included. These fundamentalist and extremist influences typically have a strong political connection and agenda. It is my opinion that the church, which for me is the Salvation Army, has the responsibility to resist the agenda being captured by the extremists and to avoid being manipulated for a political purpose.

In the world today, conflict and violence—especially with a religious connection—are a basic common concern. Personal encounters and the experience of our common humanity with our similar concerns and hopes for the future begin to transform the 'human race' into a 'human family'.

Isaiah 1:17 says: 'Seek justice, encourage the oppressed.' The history of the Salvation Army demonstrates that it has encouraged and provided for the oppressed. Through its social services it has developed expertise and fulfilled its mission to 'meet human needs in Christ's name without discrimination', providing an accepting place for people to be. In this it has obeyed the command in Isaiah. However, a small but important footnote, to be found in the New International Version, reads 'Seek justice, I rebuke the oppressor'. And so it is my conclusion that the challenge for the church in the twenty-first century is to be a prophetic voice that speaks forth the word of God, and challenges those social structures which enable oppression, marginalisation, poverty and exclusion. When we do this we are a sign of hope. Until the kingdom of God is again established by Jesus, we must continue to work to ensure that kingdom is present in the lives of individuals and societies.

Throughout its history the Salvation Army has been diligent in recording the words and deeds of its founders. They are a constant justice. They are a constant reminder that this is not an optional extra for Salvationists but is the cornerstone of our life in Christ. One such quote comes from Booth's final address before his death; I leave it with you as a response to the Key Challenges for the Church in the twenty-first century:

> What shall we do? Content ourselves by singing a hymn. Offering a prayer. Or giving a little good advice? No. Ten thousand times, no. We will forgive them, feed them, reclaim them, and employ them. Perhaps we shall fail with many. Quite likely. But our business is to help them all avail. And that is the most practical, economical, and Christ-like manner.[11]

---

11. 'Sermon: Don't Forget. An address by the late General Booth, founder of The Salvation Army', in Classic Recordings by VTM 1910.

Forum for Theology in the World Vol 1 No 2/2014

Social Concerns and Vatican II: A Response from the Catholic Tradition

Max Vodola

I am delighted to be here this morning as a representative of the Catholic tradition to give this response to Fr Frank Brennan's keynote address. I am sure it will be part of a rich, diverse and stimulating conversation in terms of Christian social thinking from our respective traditions and theological perspectives. I have recently concluded a twelve week lecture period at Catholic Theological College, East Melbourne, tracing some of the key features of the Reformation and early-modern period right up to the threshold of the Second Vatican Council (1962-65). In this Church history survey course, we pride ourselves on sometimes covering one century every fifty minutes! As I guide students through some significant periods in Church history, they invariably take a particular interest in the pontificate of Pope Leo XIII (1878-1903) and his landmark social encyclical of 1891 *Rerum Novarum*[1], the cornerstone of Catholic social teaching.[2]

The students are interested in the fact that in response to the Industrial Revolution, a pope using the teaching instrument of an encyclical[3] was, for the first time in modern history, giving a social, cultural, economic and political phenomenon a fundamentally

---

1. 'Rerum Novarum Encyclical Letter of Pope Leo XIII on Capital and Labor May 15, 1891' in *The Papal Encyclicals 1878-1903* compiled by Claudia Carlen (Wilmington, NC: McGrath Publishing Company, 1981), 241-261.
2. Bruce Duncan, *The Church's Social Teaching from Rerum Novarum to 1931* (Melbourne: Collins Dove, 1991) and John Molony, *The Worker Question: a New Historical Perspective on Rerum Novarum* (Melbourne: Collins Dove, 1991).
3. On the sophisticated development and increased use of the encyclical by popes of the nineteenth century, in particular Leo XIII, see John O'Malley, *What Happened at Vatican II* (Cambridge, MA: The Belknap Press of Harvard University Press, 2008), 52-64.

theological interpretation. The students notice that while a papal encyclical normally canvasses issues of faith and morals and the mystery of salvation, *Rerum Novarum* concerns itself in a particular way with issues such as the just wage, appropriate working conditions, the dignity of human labour, the right to form trade unions, the mutual responsibility of workers and employers, the enormous poverty of the masses and the duties of the state.[4] In addition, while the Catholic Church resisted many of the intellectual forces of the Enlightenment, the French Revolution and nineteenth century Liberalism, *Rerum Novarum* signaled a need for the Church to enter into some form of *dialogue* with the changing milieu of the time; not just a critique of the changing milieu but a dialogue which, of course, paved the way for a different theological methodology at the Second Vatican Council.[5] *Rerum Novarum* was not a 'one-hit wonder' for the Catholic Church. It laid firm foundations for the development of Catholic social teaching throughout the course of the twentieth century, to the landmark Second Vatican Council and beyond.

Christian social thinking for Australia: making a difference? I know that this is a rhetorical question but I answer it in the affirmative. On 26 October 2013, I joined Fr Bruce Duncan at Yarra Theological Union, Box Hill, for a study day on the legacy of the late Cardinal Joseph Cardijn (1882-1967)[6] and the Young Christian Workers (YCW) in Australia.[7] As a young priest, Cardijn was inspired by *Rerum Novarum* to address the changed working conditions of young Catholics especially after World War 1, the rapid secularisation and de-Christianisation of Europe and the mass exodus of young working Catholics from the traditional practice of the faith at local parish level.[8]

---

4. *Rerum Novarum*, 241-261.
5. In his magisterial work already cited, O'Malley makes the point that Vatican II used a different 'rhetoric' or style of discourse. The council fathers at Vatican II deliberately avoided the condemnatory language of previous councils with multiple *anathema sits*, in favour of what O'Malley calls a more invitational mode of discourse that he describes as epideictic or panegyric in style. O'Malley, *What Happened at Vatican II*, 307.
6. Marguerite Fievez and Jacques Meert, *Cardijn* translated by E Mitchinson (London: Young Christian Workers, 1974).
7. Breda Phillips, *More Prophetic Than We Knew: A History of the YCW in the Diocese of Sandhurst*. (Bendigo, Vic: Breda Phillips, 1999).
8. Joseph Cardijn, *Challenge to Action* edited by Eugene Langdale (Melbourne: Geoffrey Chapman, 1955).

To bridge this gap, Cardijn developed the method of 'see, judge and act'; examine the situation before you, judge it in the light of the gospel and perform some practical action that changes or ameliorates the situation. Through the YCW, which formed part of the wider organisational strategy known as Catholic Action, Cardijn instilled in his young workers an appreciation of the dignity of work, their active membership of the Church by virtue of Baptism and Confirmation and an authentic and mature lay Christian spirituality. This authentic Christian spirituality was to be manifested in the workplace in the concrete reality of daily life, as opposed to seeing lay people as some poor imitation of the priestly and religious vocation.[9] Many of the ideas and methods which Cardijn established through the YCW would come to fruition at the Second Vatican Council. Vatican II would have much to say about the call to social justice as an indispensable dimension of the Gospel of Jesus Christ, the unique nature of the lay vocation, the universal call to holiness of all the baptised in terms of mission and evangelisation and the ecumenical efforts needed to transform 'the temporal order' according to the values of God's kingdom.[10]

Catholic social teaching

Fr Frank Brennan has described Catholic social teaching as 'prophetic, pedagogical and practical'. While the YCW is no longer numerically strong in Australia as it once was, it did produce an extraordinary group of leaders and advocates (both lay and ordained) who have

---

9. Cardijn was a powerful and inspiring speaker. In an address to young workers he stated, 'It is not your business to imitate priests and religious. You are lay people, young workers, engaged couples, tomorrow, fathers, wives, mothers. The worker's tools stand in his hand as the chalice and paten in the hands of the priest ... It is not a question in the factory of having a rosary or missal in one's hands. In the factory the tools of the job are in one's hands. You have to work; but you have to also learn a spirituality in which one's work becomes one's prayer.' Quoted in Max Vodola, *Simonds: A Rewarding Life* (Melbourne: Catholic Education Office, 1997), 13.
10. *Vatican Council II: Constitutions, Decrees and Declarations* edited by Austin Flannery (Northport, NY: Costello Publishing Company, 1996). The key documents of Vatican II that refer to the unique place of laity in the life of the Church are *Lumen Gentium* (Dogmatic Constitution on the Church), *Gaudium et Spes* (Pastoral Constitution on the Church in the Modern World) and *Apostolicam Actuositatem* (Decree on the Apostolate of Lay People).

been marked for life by this method and formation and are totally committed to the work of social justice in its manifest forms. They are individuals who advocate a strong presence for the Church in the public square. But they also share this conviction with other Catholics, both lay and ordained, who advocate a more strident 'evangelical', highly confessional and sometimes militant approach to many of the pressing social, moral and ethical issues that Fr Brennan canvassed in his paper.[11] This type of advocacy, I believe, is the result of modern Christianity's own 'culture wars' which are symptomatic of the culture wars happening in wider society. Speaking from a Catholic perspective, it is very hard for our social teaching tradition to be 'prophetic, pedagogical and practical', in dialogue with the rapidly changing context of modern culture, when, to echo Fr Brennan's remarks, 'Catholics can't even talk with each other'. I think the culture wars have inflicted major casualties on the Church and this undermines our confidence and intellectual capacity to articulate a coherent social teaching message. At their worst, the culture wars look like infants quarrelling in the playground. The task of dialogue between faith and culture is a little difficult to undertake when there is not much dialogue happening within the confines of an ecclesial community.

As Fr Brennan has mentioned, the Catholic Church is suffering under the weight and shame of the international media scrutiny given to the issue of child sexual abuse by clergy. The Catholic Church and wider society are being called to account over the appalling handling of this issue over many decades. It is the perfect stick for secularists to use against Catholics in order to marginalise the Christian voice or presence in society. We must simply be honest, truly contrite and on bended knee beg the victims and their families for forgiveness once again. We did down-play the monstrously evil and simply criminal nature of these offences. We doubted the victims' stories because of our collective and institutionalised position of 'denial'. Offending priests were moved from parish to parish by some incompetent bishops who tried to avoid the issue of scandal. The greater scandal, of course, was the cover-up. It is very hard for the Catholic Church to speak about

---

11. On this, see George Weigel, *Soul of the World: Notes on the Future of Public Catholicism* (Grand Rapids, MI: Eerdmans Publishing Company, 1996) and *Evangelical Catholicism: Deep Reform in the 21st-century Church* (New York: Basic Books, 2013).

issues of justice when there is a long-standing and pressing justice issue at our own front door.[12] As Fr Brennan has noted, sometimes it is the state or civil society which provides a corrective or a further spur to the Church to be true to its finest ideals.

On the positive side of the ledger, we are all encouraged by the refreshingly new style of Pope Francis whose infectiously pastoral attitude is striking and very disarming. Don't be fooled; remember, he is a Jesuit! It is no longer 'business as usual' for the Catholic Church because in Pope Francis we find that 'the mode is the message'. He has deliberately avoided so many of the 'hot-button' issues of the culture wars in the Catholic Church going back not just to the event of the Second Vatican Council but the ongoing battle of the Council's meaning, significance and legacy.[13] Pope Francis wants a Church that is less focused on itself and more missionary. He has adopted a style of leadership that continues to dispense with established Vatican protocol and centuries-old procedures. His style is less formal and more in harmony with his inspirational choice of name, St Francis of Assisi.

Given that for Pope Francis 'the mode is the message', I think that one of the reasons his style is so appealing is that he is a 'walking, talking' social justice statement that leaves a deep impression. The Pope's words have immediate impact using clear, simple and direct language. Whenever I undertake the ritual cleaning-out of the fridge in my residence, the Pope's haunting words echo in my ears, 'Whenever we throw out food, we are taking it from the mouths of the poor'.[14]

---

12. The Victorian Parliamentary Inquiry into the Handling of Child Abuse by Religious and Other Organisations was tabled on 13 November 2013. At the time of writing, the national Royal Commission into Institutional Responses to Child Sexual Abuse was still under way.
13. Massimo Faggioli, *Vatican II: The Battle for Meaning* (Mahwah, NJ: Paulist Press, 2012). Faggioli is a graduate of the 'Bologna school', the John XXIII Foundation for Religious Studies in Bologna which published the magisterial five-volume *History of Vatican II* (1995-2006). This more progressive view of the Second Vatican Council is challenged by Agostino Marchetto, *The Second Vatican Ecumenical Council: a Counter-point for the History of the Council* (Scranton, PA: University of Scranton Press, 2010).
14. Pope Francis made this statement during his General Audience on 5 June 2013 which coincided with the United Nations World Environment Day. <www.vatican.va/.../francesco/.../papa-francesco_20130605_udienza-gen...> *Accessed on 14 January 2014.*

Read some of the statistics of social commentator Clive Hamilton[15] on the amount of food we waste every year, clothes we buy that we never wear, books we never read, CDs we never listen to, DVDs we never watch and more and more storage facilities rented for things we will probably never use again. I think social justice principles have something to say here in an era of rampant consumerism, blatant exploitation of the planet's finite natural resources and the growing gap around the world between rich and poor.[16]

Catholic social teaching: style and substance

But how does one match the new papal 'style' with the substance of a coherent, effective and ongoing Christian voice in the public square? This brings up a vexed issue for the Catholic Church. Are bishops and priests the only competent people to speak out on behalf of, or in the name of, the Church? Is there a coherent Catholic position on all moral and ethical matters in the public square? Fifty years after the Second Vatican Council, Catholics are quick to speak about the authentic place of lay leadership in the life of the Church. The only problem is that Catholics have not worked out what exactly lay leadership looks like![17] In the recent discussions about possible reforms of the Roman Curia and a greater voice for women in the Church, one incidental fact is quite revealing. The Vatican dicastery in Rome that looks after bishops and diocesan governance is called the Congregation for Bishops. There is also a similar dicastery called the Congregation for the Clergy. Fifty years after the Second Vatican Council, lay people are looked after by a department called the Pontifical Council for the Laity, one rung below the others. I think this says it all.

---

15. Clive Hamilton, *Affluenza: When Too Much is Never Enough*. (Sydney: Allen & Unwin, 2005).
16. Bruce Duncan, *Social Justice: Fuller Life in a Fairer World* (Melbourne: Garratt Publishing, 2012)
17. For a fascinating account of the emergence of a specific lay consciousness in the Catholic Church long before the Second Vatican Council, see Rosemary Goldie, *From a Roman Window* (Melbourne: Harper Collins Religious, 1998). Goldie was born in Sydney in 1916, studied Catholic theology, participated in the First World Congress on the Lay Apostolate in 1951, was one of the first female auditors (observers) at the Second Vatican Council and in 1967 was appointed by Pope Paul VI as Undersecretary of the Pontifical Council of the Laity.

The Catholic Church in Australia has a very rich and proud history of social justice statements issued by the bishops[18], of diocesan agencies promoting praiseworthy justice projects, sometimes of an ecumenical nature, and a diverse group of lay leaders, theologically literate and competent, who remain a largely untapped resource. But across the globe, the voice of lay people continues to rise up and call the Church to truly honour them and their gifts. Although to many it seems like 'ancient history', I still think that the Catholic Church in Australia has not quite got over the Labor Split of 1955.[19] One of the contributing factors to the split was a serious debate in terms of how baptised lay Catholics can authentically live out their unique vocation 'in the world' and the transformation of the temporal order beyond the confines of their traditional parish community. Many of the unresolved questions of the Split relate to the extent that Catholics, as Catholics, are able to engage in temporal affairs. To what extent are they 'representing' the Church or 'acting' in the name of the Church? To what extent are they to act on their own initiative or must they always be directed in some official manner by the hierarchy?

In the 1950s, two conflicting Catholic worldviews clashed in a volatile social, religious and political context. Many of the underlying issues of that time are still with us and will not go away, especially the issue of the Church's moral and ethical voice in the public square. In a regular lecture on the place of Catholics in public life, some of my students have often expressed alarm at Catholic parliamentarians passing legislation not in accord with official Church teaching. I ask the students to reflect on the fact that while it is a moral and ethical dilemma to have a certain proportion of Catholic parliamentarians passing legislation contrary to established Church teaching, an even greater dilemma would be if these Catholic parliamentarians were not present in our legislative chambers in the first place.[20]

---

18. Michael Hogan, *Justice Now! Social Justice Statements of the Australian Catholic Bishops 1940-1966* (Sydney: University of Sydney, 2006).
19. Bruce Duncan, *Crusade or Conspiracy? Catholics and the Anti-Communist Struggle in Australia* (Sydney: University of New South Wales Press, 2001), remains the most comprehensive account of the Catholic Church's involvement in the Labor split of 1955. See also, Brian Costar (editor), *The Great Labor Schism: A Retrospective* (Melbourne: Scribe Publications, 2005) and Gerard Henderson, *Mr Santamaria and the Bishops* (Sydney: St Patrick's College, 1982).
20. Readers may recall the 2004 US presidential campaign of Senator John Kerry

A healthy democracy needs to be on the alert for any type of political process that eliminates or 'screens-out' particular cultural or religious voices from the legislative and political arena of public life. This issue pops up occasionally in Australia where a controversial legislative proposal on euthanasia, embryonic stem-cell research or controversial medication such as RU–486 is hotly debated in the media. An atheist member of parliament proudly declares that no church, religion, bible or religious leader will influence their particular vote. The underlying motivating factors shaping the voting decision are clear. On the other hand, a Christian member of parliament feels the subtle pressure to 'check' their religious faith at the door of the legislative chamber because these motivating factors somehow have no place in shaping one's decision and worldview.[21]

I think the greatest challenge for Catholic social teaching is not the number of papal encyclicals or statements by national bishops' conferences but the tone and nature of the action that comes from social teaching as debated in the public square. It is the competence of the hierarchy to define, shape and interpret Catholic social teaching according to the various levels of authority legitimately operating in the Church, for example, conciliar teaching, papal encyclical, apostolic exhortation, canon law, Vatican instructions, pastoral letters of bishops, etc. On the other hand, it is the competence of lay people to live this out in the concrete and sometimes turbulent reality of public life, ethical debate, higher education, popular culture, the media, the parliament and the judiciary.

According to Vatican II's document on the Church (*Lumen Gentium* no. 35), the laity are called to be powerful heralds of the

---

who, as a Catholic, stated that he was personally against abortion but because of the separation of church and state felt that his religious faith could not be the standard by which he legislated for the country. An interesting situation arose whereby some American bishops publicly announced that they would refuse Kerry holy communion whereas other bishops stated that this was a matter of conscience and that the sacrament of the eucharist was not to be used as a partisan weapon in times of highly charged political debate such as a presidential campaign.

21. On the place of religion in Australian public life see the helpful studies of Brian Howe and Philip Hughes, *Spirit of Australia II: religion in citizenship and national life* (Adelaide: ATF Press, 2003) and Marion Maddox, *God and Howard: The Rise of the Religious Right in Australian Politics* (Sydney: Allen & Unwin, 2005).

faith. This is the task of evangelisation. 'This evangelisation—that is, the proclamation of Christ by word and the witness of their lives—acquires a special character and a particular effectiveness because it is accomplished in the ordinary circumstances of the world'. These are not accidental words chosen by the bishops at Vatican II. By 'special character' and 'particular effectiveness', the bishops at Vatican II said something quite specific about the unique and proper domain where lay people give witness to the life of faith. It is proper to them by virtue of their baptism and their universal call to holiness and mission. It is the domain of family life, the economy, work, culture, the media, commercial life, education, the field of ecumenical endeavour and participation in all other public and civic institutions. It is rightly beyond the walls of the sacristy. This is where Catholic social teaching belongs and comes to life and where it will continue to make a difference. It has a special character and a particular effectiveness and is needed now more than ever.[22]

As Fr Brennan has noted, religion cannot provide all the answers to complex questions of law, politics and the economy. However, religious faith and religious traditions can make a significant contribution to debate in the public square, shaping and informing the relevant issues from a diversity of perspectives as opposed to implementing some former vision of a unified church and state. The deliberate (and pastoral) strategy of the Catholic bishops at the Second Vatican Council was to enter into dialogue with the rapidly changing social, cultural, religious and political milieux of the time, a time which Pope John XXIII (1958-63) discerned as a new historical epoch for the Church and the world.[23] The task of the Council was to

---

22. In her book Rosemary Goldie quotes American lay activist Martin Work, 'If lay people have a myopic vision of the Church, and of their own roles, are they altogether to blame? We were educated as 'pew-sitters', then shoved into the aisle as collectors and ushers, hired as sacristans … and now we are being pushed into the jungle of the temporal world, where we should have been all along'. Goldie, *From a Roman Window*, 58.
23. The text of Pope John XXIII's opening address at the Council on 11 October 1962 can be found in Jared Wicks, *Doing Theology* (Mahwah, NJ: Paulist Press, 2009), 141-151. Wicks refers to John XXIII's opening speech as Vatican II's 'first great text'.

seek out and foster positions of mutuality, not just within the Catholic tent, but to go beyond to people of other Christian traditions, other religious traditions and those of no ostensible tradition, to all men and women of goodwill. It was a new paradigm for the Catholic Church and it continues to shape our social teaching tradition.

Forum for Theology in the World Vol 1 No 2/2014

Social Thinking Among Churches of Christ in Australia

Gerald Rose

In this article I first address some of the key issues pertaining to the historical position taken by Churches of Christ in Australia in relation to social action. After illustrating the dilemma that has bedevilled this religious body's approach to contentious social issues, I will outline the theological and ecclesiological reasons for this dilemma. Second, I will then examine the emerging legal situation pertaining to social ethics in contemporary Western society. Finally I will relate this to the cultural change that has reshaped Western society and examine critical challenges in social praxis confronting all churches in the current social and cultural context.

Churches of Christ historical position

The framing of a dilemma: a case study
The origins of what is widely referred to as 'The Restoration Movement' within the 'radical left wing' of Protestantism[1] profoundly influenced the Australian Churches of Christ and shaped their attitude to social wellbeing and issues related to justice. This background has left them with a major dilemma in developing a corporate response on these issues and a challenge to the historian to trace the diversity of their responses.

The dilemma for Churches of Christ is that both their theology and ecclesiology have limited their ability to have a unified voice, particularly in matters pertaining to social justice.

---

1. Harold L Lunger, *The Political Ethics of Alexander Campbell* (St Louis, MO: The Bethany Press, 1954), 17-18.

Yet, despite this background, Churches of Christ (particularly in South Australia and Victoria) have not only had a strong ecumenical engagement but have found ways of contributing to social welfare and engaging in social justice issues.

The following is an example of the dilemma the denomination has faced in providing a voice for, and giving guidance to, its churches and their congregants on major social issues. A motion was passed at the Federal Conference of Churches of Christ in 1977 in response to the findings of the Royal Commission on Human Relationships (1974-1977). After congratulating the Commission for the 'diligence, integrity and scholarship' of the Royal Commission's findings, urging the member churches of the denomination to study carefully its findings and urging that 'studies be made of the problems involved in the adequate provision of appropriate sex education in the community', the motion continues:

> Understanding that the Christian ethic is accepted by individuals as an outcome of their Christian faith, and understanding that the Christian ethic could not and should not be imposed on others by legislation or other forms of compulsion, this Conference notes the Royal Commission's proposal that sexual practices as are privately engaged in by consenting adults be decriminalised. At the same time, this Conference urges our churches to continue to encourage all people to conduct themselves at all times in ways consistent with the Christian faith and Christian principles as revealed in the scriptures.[2]

This last clause of the motion effectively goes nowhere in terms of shaping or giving guidance to its members or other interested persons other than to affirm that the Christian ethic cannot be legislated—a proposal that in any case the Commission was not suggesting. How can a religious body that has produced outstanding contributors

---

2. Graeme Chapman, *No Other Foundation: A Documentary History of Churches of Christ in Australia*, volume III (Melbourne: privately published, undated), 744, quoting a report in the *Australian Christian*, 87 (1977): 93.

to community wellbeing, fail to engage at depth with such a major document in Australian public life?

The dilemma for the denomination in providing such guidance is that even motions passed by the Federal Conference or a State Conference are not binding on either individual congregations or congregants and any attempt to make a statement on behalf of the whole body is all but impossible as those churches dissenting from it are able simply to ignore it.

This however does not mean that Churches of Christ have been totally absent from either public debate or action to alleviate social needs or to advocate on behalf of those suffering deprivation. But where this has happened it has largely been at the initiative of individuals or groups who, at least initially, were not acting officially on behalf of the denomination.

Churches of Christ and community concern
Churches of Christ have contributed widely to social causes but mainly through the action and/or influence of individuals. For example, they have contributed richly to political life. One of the early Premiers of Victoria (1880, 1883-6), James Service, was the son of Robert Service, one of the pioneers of the 'Restoration Movement' in Victoria. Sir Douglas Nicholls, former Governor of South Australia and pioneer advocate for his kindred indigenous people, was a Churches of Christ pastor. Three of the founders of the first Church of Christ in Australia all became members of the South Australian parliament in the 1800s. In the twentieth century, members of Churches of Christ have been elected to the Federal Parliament and to all of the State parliaments. In respect to social issues and interfaith dialogue, E Lyall Williams, former Principal of the federal theological college of Churches of Christ in Australia, was a major contributor to both the peace and the ecumenical movements. The first Secretary and the last two Executive Officers of the Victorian Council of Churches have been graduates of the Churches of Christ federal theological college. In medicine, the South Australian Sir Philip Messent, Director General of Surgical Studies at Adelaide University and a surgeon to the Queen, was President of the World Convention of Restoration Movement churches held in Adelaide in 1970.[3]

---

3. A little known fact is that world-renowned eye surgeon, Fred Hollows,

But collectively the story is less clear-cut. The explanation for this lies in our origins in the radical left wing of Protestantism. To explain this I will outline the life and thought of Alexander Campbell whose writings crystallised for many the intentions of the widespread Restoration Movement which, in the middle decades of the nineteenth century, gave rise to the Australian Churches of Christ.

Origins of the Australian Churches of Christ
Churches of Christ are a product of the European religious and cultural environment in the early 1800s. Alexander Campbell (1788–1866) and his father Thomas Campbell (1763–1854) are key figures in the development of the ideas that shaped our movement. Father and son shared a vision of a unified church based on the restoration of the pattern of church polity and faith they identified in the pages of the New Testament. Originally from Ireland, they emigrated to the United States where they formulated their vision for the church. The writings of Alexander in particular influenced and gave shape to what was largely an inchoate 'restoration movement' emerging in a number of countries around the world.

The founders of Churches of Christ in Australia were immigrants from England, Scotland and Ireland. While being strongly influenced by the writings of the Campbells (recycled through British periodicals), they nonetheless created within the Australian movement a distinctive ethos reflecting their backgrounds in various independent and Scotch Baptist churches in the United Kingdom. Even so, they identified themselves as part of that same world-wide 'restoration movement' that, along with the Campbells and others in the USA, was seeking to restore the faith and practices of the 'primitive church' of the New Testament.

The Campbellite Heritage
As one biographer has noted, 'Alexander Campbell can be best understood against the background of the "ideal type" of left wing Protestantism classically exemplified by the Anabaptists and Spiritual Reformers of sixteenth century Europe'.[4]

---

commenced his tertiary academic career as a student in the Glen Leith Bible College, the theological seminary of Churches of Christ in New Zealand.

4. Lunger, *The Political Ethics*, 17.

The four characteristics of this radical wing of the Reformation have been identified as:

> The ethical note, or the ideal of a pure church; Christian primitivism, or the attempt to restore primitive Christianity on the basis of a Biblicism of either the Old or the New Testament; a heightened sense of eschatology, which in some instances passed over to revolution but more often took the form of a passive and patient enduring of present evils while awaiting the coming of the Millennium; and the radical separation of church and state.[5]

All four elements are found in the writings of Alexander Campbell, whose periodicals *The Christian Baptist* (1823-30) and *The Millennial Harbinger* (1830-63) reflected the radical ethos of the left wing of Protestantism in the United States in the nineteenth century and which influenced the founders of Churches of Christ in Australia.

Campbell's father, Thomas, was an anti-Burgher, Old Light, Seceder Presbyterian clergyman. Each one of these descriptors represents a division in the Presbyterian Church in the late eighteenth century in Scotland and Northern Ireland. And each of those divisions related in one way or another to disputes related to the disestablishment of the State Church. In 1807 Thomas emigrated to the US leaving his family to follow him a year later.

In his father's absence, eighteen-year-old Alexander became interested in the teachings of the Independent and anti-establishment preachers and writers of the period. A year after the departure of Thomas, the family attempted to join him but their ship was wrecked on the coast of Scotland. In the year that it took for the family to refinance their voyage Alexander studied at Glasgow University. There, he was deeply influenced by the writers of the Scottish Enlightenment, particularly John Locke whose *Letters on Toleration* he had read as a boy.[6] He was also influenced by leaders of the Scottish Independence (or 'congregational') movement. When he joined his

---

5. Roland Bainton, 'The Left Wing of the Reformation', in *Journal of Religion,* xxi (April, 1941): 22-3, cited in Lunger *The Political Ethics*, 17-18.
6. Lunger, *The Political Ethics*, 22.

father in western Pennsylvania he found that Thomas had reached similar conclusions. For example, they both were convinced that the Christian church was 'essentially, intentionally and constitutionally one', and 'that nothing ought to be inculcated upon Christians as articles of faith, nor required of them as terms of communion, but what is expressly taught and enjoined upon them in the word of God'.[7] Soon after Alexander's arrival, Thomas published the 'Declaration and Address', a document drawn up by him and a group of other Christians who called themselves 'The Christian Association of PA, USA' and the formation of this group marked historically the first move of what in the USA was to become 'The Disciples of Christ'.

Over the next decade, Alexander emerged as the main spokesperson and publicist of this branch of a world-wide Restoration Movement. His writings crystallised for others in Britain and eventually in Australia and New Zealand many of the sentiments that formed the ethos of Churches of Christ.

Alexander's social ideology was aligned with the radical left of Protestantism in emphasising the individual's right to freedom of choice in politics and in religion. His ecclesiology aligned him with Christian 'primitivists' in that he held 'that nothing that was not as old as the New Testament should be made an article of faith, rule of practice or a term of communion amongst Christians'.[8] In his theology he was a post-millennialist.

Remarkably Campbell found no role for church-based activism and particularly in his early years in America, he embraced an extreme 'quietist' attitude to even individual Christians participating in political action.[9] This position was particularly congruent with his millennialism.

---

7. Thomas Campbell, *Declaration and Address* (1809), in William Robinson's *Declaration and Address: Reprinted with an Introduction by William Robinson* (Birmingham: Berean Press, 1951), 15.
8. Alexander Campbell, 'Address to the Public', in *The Christian Baptist*, 2/2 (1824): unnumbered.
9. Despite his quietism in relation to political involvement, he participated as an elected representative to the 1829-30 Virginia Constitutional Convention, explaining that he did so 'to lay a foundation for the abolition of slavery', and to give both his writings and personal standing influence to counter negative comments that were being circulated about him. Lunger, commenting on the seeming inconsistency of his participation, writes, 'As a constitutionalist and believer in government by laws rather than by men, he felt at liberty to debate and determine the fundamental principles of government, even though he kept aloof from partisan politics'. Lunger, *The Political Ethics*, 77.

There were two interpretations of how the millennial period described in Revelation 20:1-3 would come about. Those who believed that the final advent of Christ would precede the millennium saw the world prior to that event getting worse and worse. The task of the church prior to the final Advent was to rescue as many sinners as possible so that they would not suffer the fate of the condemned. In terms of social action for justice, they were extreme quietists as they saw such activity as a distraction from the church's main task of saving the souls of sinners.

Others, of whom Campbell was one, believed that the millennium would precede the return of Christ and that the world would get better and better as the millennium approached. He wrote:

> The Millennium . . . will be a state of greatly enlarged and continuous prosperity, in which the Lord will be exalted and his divine spirit enjoyed to an unprecedented measure. All the conditions of society will be vastly improved; wars will cease, and peace and good will among men will generally abound. Genuine Christianity will be diffused through all nations; crimes and punishments will cease; governments will recognise human rights, and will rest on just and benevolent principles . . . [There will be] one extended and protracted series of revivals . . . [and even] the seasons will become mild; climate more salubrious, health more vigorous, labour less, lands more fertile, and the animal creation more prolific.[10]

In the USA at this time there was ample evidence to support the belief that human conditions were improving and this reinforced the conviction that the millennium was on the way. But while this post-millennial position led to a less extreme form of quietism by allowing some scope for human activity in ameliorating social evils, it none the less made it plain that the improving conditions were actually the result of divine rather than human activity.

---

10. Alexander Campbell, in *The Millennial Harbinger*, (1841): 9; quoted in Lunger, *The Political Ethics*, 55.

While throughout his life Campbell himself was very active in defending the individual's right to freedom and in resisting any form of religious establishment,[11] he felt uneasy about political involvement because of the tension between his innate quietism and his public involvement with the affairs of the State. As his own personal circumstances and that of his fellow restorationists in the USA steadily improved, he became less radical but this only confirmed his conviction that religious service was more important than service to the State.[12]

While the millennial motif no longer plays any major role in the thinking of churches associated with the Restoration Movement, a pattern had been established.

Throughout their history in Australia, Churches of Christ main activities in social affairs have related to public morality and the care of the needy rather than advocating for social justice and societal change. In the period prior to World War I the social issues focused on the consumption of alcohol, dancing, the theatre, gambling, and Sunday observance. Where broader policy issues such as socialism and the churches' relationship with the emerging Labor Party were discussed the emphasis fell upon the need for the individual Christian to take action. FG Dunn, editor of the *Australian Christian* in 1907 wrote:

> The churches as churches are not a political factor. Any political power is exercised through the individual and each individual selects his own politics. It is only in questions that relate to morals that the church can be said to be a unit in so far as the State is concerned.[13]

---

11. During the mid-1800s, Campbell's fame as a public debater in defence of individual rights and an advocate for freedom of choice in religion spread throughout the United States so that his name became known in most households across the country.
12. It is interesting to note that in the Australian context James Service faced the same dilemma but his life took the opposite course. Commencing in his early days in Melbourne as a fiery and zealous evangelist, as his circumstances in life improved greatly through his business interests, he moved away from the church and became one of the most influential Victorian politicians in the second half of the nineteenth century.
13. FG Dunn, 'The Churches and Labor', in *The Australian Christian*, (1907): 640-

Some seventy years later, E Lyall Williams, former Principal of the College of the Bible, while reaffirming this stance sought to extend the role of the corporate body of the church in action for social justice.

> The church as a prophetic community cannot withdraw or be silent in any area of community life. As a prophetic community it will be concerned with justice beyond the niceties of charity. Its prophetic task will be performed by producing concerned citizens who seek to live out the Gospel in all areas of life where they find themselves and as a corporate and responsible body exposing all evils in the light of Christian truth.[14]

But while individuals within the denomination have continued to speak and act on social justice issues, the corporate response of the denomination has been muted. On the other hand, Churches of Christ have contributed extensively in welfare-related ministries.

From individual actions to corporate organisation
The early impetus for welfare ventures came from the independent action of individuals, often lay women, acting independently from local congregational or Conference structures. For example, in Victoria one of the early initiatives (1890) was the establishment of a 'rescue home' for 'unfortunate women' (prostitutes). This was followed by a second home, this time for women at risk of becoming prostitutes. Around the same time, the Burwood Boys home was established. Each of these projects was established by concerned individuals and then run by independent committees of concerned lay volunteers.[15]

From 1895 the various State Conferences established Social Service committees. These committees emerged from Temperance

---

1; quoted in Graeme Chapman, *No other foundation*, volume. II, (Melbourne: privately published, undated), 450.
14. E Lyall Williams, *Living Responsibly* (Melbourne: Vital Publications, undated), 92.
15. AB Maston, *Jubilee Pictorial History of Churches of Christ in Australasia* (Melbourne: Austral Publishing, 1903), 174.

committees.[16] By the 1920s the provenance of the Social Service Committees had expanded to embrace food assistance for the poor, work for the unemployed, housing for migrants, the wellbeing of prisoners and care for the aged. This expansion led in turn to State Conferences establishing and funding Social Services departments. Initially these departments simply coordinated congregational activities but soon became responsible for the funding and running of state-wide welfare programs.

In Victoria the layman CR Burdeau, a member of the State Conference Executive, had personally taken over the supervision of a program providing food for the impoverished that had been initiated by the Burnley congregation. In 1924, this program was incorporated into the newly formed Social Services Department under Burdeau's leadership.[17] In 1926, Will Clay was appointed the Director of this Department and under his skilled leadership Churches of Christ in Victoria developed a range of welfare activities including Aged Care Homes and a hospital. Clay himself engaged in a wide range of State and community activities as well as becoming a strong advocate of social justice. During this same period (1920-1950) development in the other State Conferences in Australia followed a similar trajectory.

Social justice and ecclesial structures

A major factor contributing to the problem of finding a unified voice on social justice issues has been a fierce commitment to the independence of the local congregation and the consequent 'flat' ecclesial structure Churches of Christ have embraced.[18] This has made it very difficult for any representative body, such as State or

---

16. Graeme Chapman, *One Lord, One Faith, One Baptism: a History of Churches of Christ in Australia* (Melbourne: Vital Publications, 1979), 87.
17. At that time Burdeau was a senior clerk in the governmental pensions department. Chapman comments:
    He later went to New South Wales and then Queensland (where) he gave a fillip to social services in those States . . . The Federal Government appointed him Queensland Director of Social Services, Commonwealth Government, and later Australian Assistant Director of Social Services, Commonwealth Government.
    Chapman, *One Lord, One Faith, One Baptism,* 109.
18. There is no equivalent position within the framework of Churches of Christ to that of a bishop. Historically within the Movement that role has been filled by the editors of various journals published within the Restoration Movement across the world.

Federal Conference, to speak authoritatively as the voice representing Churches of Christ official positions on social or justice issues. The closely guarded independence of the local congregation has meant that no congregation can ultimately be bound even to those decisions agreed upon by Conference. Where a measure of consensus has been achieved it has related to issues of personal morality. However, in more recent times, as these issues have become more contentious, the consensus over appropriate Christian mores has dissipated. Consequently, the denomination can make only limited statements on important social issues such as the findings of the Royal Commission on Social Relations referred to above.

The emerging situation
Following the 'religious crisis of the 1960s'[19] there was a period of heightened activity at State and Federal Conferences where various motions related to social justice were presented and usually passed but little activity either by Conference officials or local congregations followed. In Victoria, with the founding of the Social Justice Network of Churches of Christ in Victoria and Tasmania in 2000, there was another flurry of motions passed at the State Conference. However the major outcome of the Network's activity was the establishing of a webpage[20] and blog[21] where articles related to social justice were made available for churches and individuals to consult.

In recent years in Victoria and Tasmania, the focus of the Community Care Department of Churches of Christ has shifted from the provision of aged care to enabling local congregations to become actively involved in meeting the social needs of their communities through the development and conduct of benevolent programs primarily through local congregations.

However, the continuing problems for the denomination in relation to action for social justice remain essentially theological and ecclesiological. Where the denomination's major concern is focused on evangelism, conceived basically as the 'saving of souls' for

---

19. D Hilliard, 'The Religious Crisis of the 1960s: The Experience of the Australian Churches' in *Journal of Religious History*, 21 (1997): 209-227.
20. <http://www.cofcsjn.org.au>.
21. http://www.churchesofchristsocialjusticenetwork.blogspot.com.au>. As of 2014, this and the website above are no longer active.

a kingdom of God which is beyond this mortal life and practising benevolence as an expression of Christian love, there will continue to be difficulties with actively pursuing issues related to justice and the empowering of the marginalised and disenfranchised in this world. This approach fails to recognise the significance of the destructive influence of the 'principalities and powers' experienced through corruption and destructive social forces. Churches of Christ still struggle to play a significant role as a Christian body in bringing wholeness to all aspects of human life and environmental wellbeing.

In his review of the literature related to the provision of community services and the role of Christian providers, Hughes, referencing Cleary,[22] writes 'If the church is truly about the Kingdom of God, then "the church and its leaders cannot afford not to engage in the politics of civil life".[23] Without a thoroughly biblical theology of the Kingdom of God, Churches of Christ will lack the necessary vision of human society and its physical environment to realise their full potential for good.

Among the Ministers of Churches of Christ participating in a recent research project,[24] it was particularly those engaged in intentionally 'incarnational' ministry who articulated that doing the work of the Kingdom of God meant engaging in the reformation of the structures of society. However, this insight was often obscured by their commitment to making converts.

A major issue for all denominations, including Churches of Christ, is to engage with the fundamental change occurring in Western culture and how this has reshaped society. This change has implications for all the major social institutions of society, including the religious, governmental and legislative sectors. This shift is already affecting how the legal system is interpreting its role in respect to civic morality. This has significant implications for how the churches can effectively advocate for social justice and community well-being.

---

22. Ray Cleary, 'The church and civil society: mission imperatives', in *Church and Civil Society: a Theology of Engagement*, edited by F Sullivan and S Leppert (Adelaide: ATF Press, 2004).
23. Philip Hughes, *History and Theology of Christian Welfare in Australia: A Review of the Literature* (Melbourne: Christian Research Association and MCD University of Divinity, 2013), 8.
24. Gerald Rose, *Re-imagining Church: Creating Sacred Spaces for the Experience of the Sacred in an Evolving Experiential Culture*, A thesis submitted for the award of Doctor of Philosophy through Monash University, Clayton. Awarded 2013.

Religion, law and the experiential shift in post-secular western culture

A critical factor that is impacting upon the ability of the Christian church to shape public opinion on issues related to social wellbeing and justice has been a fundamental shift in Western culture.[25] This relates specifically to the basis on which individuals, organisations and social institutions (such as the legal system) make important decisions.

Sir James Munby[26] in an address delivered at the Family Law Annual Conference in London on 29 October 2013[27] identified a major cultural shift that had emerged in the 1960s and was reflected in a number of Acts of the British Parliament and in pivotal British court decisions related to sexuality. These events represented a fundamental shift from the judiciary's responsibility to preserve traditional standards of sexual morality. Instead, the standards to be used in judgements were now determined by the 'sentiments of ordinary but responsible citizens'. He wrote:

> Today, surely, the judicial task is to assess matters by the standards of reasonable men and women in 2013—not, I would add, by the standards of their parents in 1970—and having regard to the ever changing nature of our world: changes in our understanding of the natural world, technological changes, changes in social standards and, perhaps most important of all, changes in social attitudes ... Within limits the law—our family law—will tolerate things which society as a whole may find undesirable.[28]

The 'unbreakable' link between a traditional moral code and the judiciary that had made judges the moral guardians of societal mores

---

25. Gary Bouma, *Australian Soul: Religion and Spirituality in the Twenty-first Century* (Melbourne: Cambridge University Press, 2006), 88ff.
26. President of the Family Division of the Law Society in the United Kingdom.
27. Sir James Munby, *The Sacred and the Secular: Religion, Culture and the Family Courts* <http://www.lawandreligionuk.com/author/kranf/>. Accessed 5 November 2013.
28. Sir James Munby, 'The Sacred and the Secular', 7-8.

has been broken. The responsibility for maintaining traditional moral standards is no longer vested in the considered (rational) judgements of a trained legal profession. Instead, they are based on the experiences and tastes of the 'reasonable' individuals who elect their representatives to frame moral standards that more or less reflect the outlook of their electors.

While this perspective can be categorised simply as 'individualism', it in fact goes much deeper. It represents a fundamental difference in the basis on which decisions are increasingly made in Western culture. Ultimately, there are only three grounds on which ultimate authority rests. Identified originally by Max Weber,[29] these grounds are 'traditional' authority ('We've always done things this way!'), 'rational instrumental' authority ('This is the way things really work and will give us the outcome we want') and 'experiential' or 'charismatic' authority located 'in the individual's experience, senses and feelings'[30] ('This feels right for me'). All three grounds of authority are available for use in any situation, but one or another will dominate in particular eras.[31]

The experiential cultural shift

We are now living in an era in which experiential authority predominates in many aspects of society. In law this can be seen at the popular level in the growth of the 'Do it yourself' (DIY) Will'. In the judicial system it can be seen in the way that social issues such as homosexuality and abortion are increasingly viewed not as criminal offences but as issues in which individuals are themselves responsible to make their own lifestyle decisions. The more overtly expressive emotional regimes characteristic of the 'permissive society' are tolerated where once they would have been regarded as

---

29. Max Weber, 'The Pure Types of Legitimate Authority', in *Max Weber On Charisma and Institution Building: Selected Papers,* edited by SN Eisenstadt (Chicago: University of Chicago Press, 1968 [1947]), 46-77.
30. Bouma, *Australian Soul*, 90.
31. Traditional authority dominated the mediaeval era and instrumental rationality began to gain dominance from the time of the Protestant Reformation (though the Churches generally opted for rationalising their traditions) and has been characteristic of modernity. Experiential authority has become characteristic of late- or high-modernity (often referred to simplistically as the period of 'post-modernity') which began to emerge in the mid-1960s.

decidedly 'unseemly'. Likewise, the overt emotionality of more recent forms of worship are condemned in 'rational authority' churches as exhibitionist and out of step with the rule that worship must be conducted 'decently and in order' (1 Cor 14:40, AV).

What is evident today is that when ordinary people, and even when society at large, is making important decisions, there is a shift away from tradition and even 'common sense' rationality to the authority of personal experience.

The church today, then, is confronted by a world in which people will not easily accept external authority that does not resonate with their personal experience. The churches where 'traditional' authority and 'rational' authority (post-Reformation religiosity) have been dominant, are not well equipped to handle this.

There is also a link between the experiential turn in the culture and a major shift in Government economic policy particularly in relation to welfare practices. The application of economic rationalism to welfare policies has diminished governmental responsibility for the care of the needy. Instead, governments have been implementing consumer-oriented, cost/benefit policies which make individual consumers responsible for their own wellbeing. In this ideology, words like 'dignity', 'self-interest' and 'self-respect' become code for the government's desire to de-regulate the market. When church bodies have opposed this policy shift, they have been advised that 'Christian discussion of public economic policy is intrusive and inherently dangerous, if it proposes interference with the mechanisms of the market'.[32] In this paradigm, the individual is left isolated with only his or her own resources to draw upon. Economic rationalism assumes every individual is responsible for his/her own wellbeing. As such it is well attuned to, and exploits, the shift to individual 'experiential' authority.

Exploring a new paradigm for action for social justice.
The church today, particularly in its advocacy for social justice, is confronted by a world different from what our traditions have led us to expect. Rational dialogue is no longer an effective instrument for dealing with the wider public. Today, we are engaging with a

---

32. Andrew Hamilton, *Alongside the Poor: the Churches Facing the Challenges?* (Melbourne: The Victorian Council of Christian Education, 1990), 23.

world where people work out of their own personal experience. Any attempt we may make to help people grasp the social justice aspects of Christianity is going to have to be clearly related to their life experiences rather than traditional beliefs or abstract rationality. But this requires an 'action/reflection' approach in dealing with public issues rather than the didactic pedagogy used in the past.

The current era is often described as a 'post-modern' age. I prefer to see it as an 'experiential'[33] and 'post-secular' era. It is a time of disillusionment with the outcomes of rationalistic scientism. This has resulted in a groundswell of the re-sacralisation of life-events and a return to spirituality.[34] A great deal of this resacralising of life-events, however, has taken an ostensibly non-Christian form. It has, if anything, been symptomatic of a rejection of authoritarian religion that fails to respect individual experience. The experiential turn in the culture has resulted in a 'new kind of subjective anarchy of belief which forms an increasingly poor fit with the dogmatic framework provided by institutionalised religions', a concept that is not contrary to Christian faith but is 'embedded in the Christian tradition itself'.[35]

In terms of advocacy of certain standards in public life, appeals to tradition or even rationality are unlikely to have anything like the effectiveness that could have been expected prior to the experiential shift in the culture. What is likely to have greater effect is where the church is seen to be compassionately concerned for those who are 'doing it tough'. Demanding conformity with the church's traditional moral norms from those who do not hold these is counter-productive

---

33. The philosopher Charles Taylor writes of a 'massive subjective turn in modern culture' in which 'each of us has an original way of being human'. Charles Taylor, *A Secular Age* (Cambridge, MA: Belknap Press of Harvard University Press, 2007), 473, and sociologists Heelas and Woodhead use the descriptor 'subjective turn' in relation to the cultural change that is shaping the emerging forms of spirituality in contemporary society. Paul Heelas and Linda Woodhead, *The Spiritual Revolution: Why Religion is Giving Way to Spirituality* (Oxford: Blackwell, 2005). Russell Sandberg in *Religion, Law and Society* (Cambridge: Cambridge University Press, 2014) examines the way the subjective is reflected in a number of European law cases related to sexual identity.
34. There is now a considerable body of research related to various aspects of the increased interest in contemporary spirituality and its relation to religiosity. (For example, see Heelas and Woodhead, *The Spiritual Revolution*, 2005).
35. Ulrich Beck, *A God of One's Own: Religion's Capacity for Peace and Potential for Violence* (Cambridge: Polity Press, 2010), 90; quoted in Sandberg, *Religion, Law and Society*, 225.

for the church. Trying to impose attitudes that are not congruent with the felt needs of individuals will seem paternalistic and/or dogmatic.

Evangelical scholar and social justice protagonist, Oz Guinness, advocates that in the public square, the contemporary church, rather than arguing, which is a waste of time, needs to pursue a strategy of persuasion because 'persuasion . . . is not imposition.'[36]

Often the way we (the churches) have talked about social justice issues has been condemnatory. Instead, we need to learn how to speak 'hope-fully' to our generation in the way that the post-Millennialism of Campbell and his associates spoke of 'plentitude, rectitude and justice' to their generation. How can we speak the Gospel (the 'good-news' of the Kingdom) in relation to public issues in ways that persuade by speaking hope instead of judgement?

In terms of seeking to bring about social change and restorative justice, active involvement with those who are the victims of society—the poor, the needy, the marginalised and those who experience injustice—provides the rich experience that inspires a form of active discipleship that is able to engage in social transformation.

As those who have been called to be agents of the Kingdom of God (and not just advocates for the church), we have an important gift to share with our contemporaries. It is the experience of transcendence, the experience of God in the many different ways that this presents itself. The recovery of the core experiential dimension of religion may well provide a more meaningful point of contact with a society described as 'hope-deficient.'[37] Reasonable explanation arising from our own experience along with clear but negotiated moral aspirations and respect for the others' experience will provide the necessary frame of meaning to engage with our contemporaries.

Conclusion

In this article I have described the dilemma Churches of Christ have experienced in relation to the implementation of social welfare and in relation to taking a denominational position on some major social issues and, in particular, advocacy and action for social

---

36. Oz Guiness, *The Global Public Square: Religious Freedom and the Making of a World Safe for Diversity* (Downers Grove, IL: IVP Press, 2013), 184.
37. Donald Miller *Re-inventing American Protestantism: Christianity in the New Millennium* (Berkeley: University of California Press, 1997), 185.

justice. Historically, their theology and ecclesiology has meant that their concern has been primarily expressed through the actions of individuals. In terms of providing social welfare across a broad spectrum of social needs, denominational programs have evolved. However, advocacy for social justice has largely been dependent upon individuals that were willing to act out of their own conscience.

The cultural shift that has been occurring in Australia in common with all Western societies has meant that the mainstream Christian denominations have found themselves in largely unfamiliar territory both in working with governmental agencies and in their role in the public square. In a number of ways, the flat organisational structures of Churches of Christ and their emphasis upon the importance of individual experience and personal responsibility for the work of Christ's kingdom may yet prove to be major assets in adjusting to the cultural shift.

Forum for Theology in the World Vol 1 No 2/2014

Social Concern in the Baptist Tradition

Geoff Pound

A kingly model

On 24 August 2013, tens of thousands of Americans gathered around the Lincoln Memorial to mark the fiftieth anniversary of the March on Washington. It was a time to look back to the march of 1963, which represented a watershed in the civil rights movement. This demonstration paved the way for the signing of the Civil Rights Act the following year, that outlawed discrimination based on race, gender and religion.

Those in the Baptist tradition, in Australia and in many parts of the world, look back with some pride to the Baptist preacher who gave a voice to the voiceless on that day, one who articulated the dream of thousands around the world who yearned for freedom.

Martin Luther King Jnr epitomises the best in the Baptist tradition when it comes to social concern. King highlights the role of prophetic preaching that arises from a deep commitment to social justice. He and his movement testify to the importance of a rigorous public theology that issues in creative social activism that may bring about changes in the law. This event calls attention to the critical need for public theologians to work closely with the churches, which can both organise people and raise money.

This recent anniversary has also reminded Baptists that Dr King shared the platform that day with speakers from various denominations and religious traditions. We recall that social thinking and social action are best done ecumenically and with all people of goodwill, regardless of their religious affiliation.

Separatist tendencies

This ecumenical co-operation has taken a long time for Baptists to develop. Baptists were part of the Separatists who broke away from the Church of England. They challenged the established Church's practice of determining the doctrine, ordering the liturgy and appointing leaders and preachers. This opposition was not only a religious act but also a political act whereby these early Baptists were asserting the freedom of religion. Fleeing England as religious refugees and finding asylum in Holland is part of the Baptist story. The prophetic challenge, the freedom of religion and the separatist tendency are strands within the Baptist DNA that affect the level of engagement and trust with others engaged in social thinking and activism.

The separatism and diversity of viewpoints divide and sometimes decimate the Baptist movement. King discovered that many of his fiercest critics were leaders of the Baptist Church. His famous 'Letter from a Birmingham Jail' was a response to Southern clergymen who criticised him for being an extremist. King observed that the most segregated hour in America was 11 o'clock on Sunday when people attended church. Proponents of social thinking from the Baptist tradition still operate within a church that is diverse and within which are their fiercest critics and enemies.

In-house focus

The protests of the group of Protestants known as 'Baptist' were historically focused upon issues of ecclesiology. Being part of the Free Church tradition, their energy was expended on in-house matters such as the correct form of baptism, the right mode of communion, the essential elements of worship and the nature of the ministry. In explaining the 'Baptist silence on public issues', Laurie Guy says that by stepping out of the arrangement where church and state were closely linked:

> Baptists conceptually were inclined to stand outside society. Their focus went much more on the individual and on the local church at the expense of a focus on society. This sort of perspective has commonly led

Baptists to focus on saving and maintaining 'souls' and planting and growing churches, without much balancing concern for the great issues of society.[1]

The challenge then and for Baptists today is to switch the focus from the church to the community, to think theologically about the church and society.

What's in a name?

Being given the nickname 'Baptist' reveals where early Baptists were seen to place their emphasis—on the mode of baptism (immersion rather than sprinkling) and on the faith requirement of the one being baptised (believer's baptism rather than infant baptism). Baptists have developed as part of the evangelical wing of the church where much attention has been focused on personal salvation expressed by the baptism of believers and the conviction that the church is comprised of believers who have received new life in Christ. While evangelism is regarded as one of the strengths of the Baptist movement, the preoccupation with how one starts to follow Jesus has led to a neglect in helping believers to go on. The stress on personal salvation has not been balanced by a commitment to salvation in its broadest dimensions, the transformation of society with a deep passion for social justice.

Domesticated Gospel

Several years ago a discussion took place between two Christian leaders in America—Billy Graham, the well known Baptist evangelist, and William Sloane Coffin, minister of the Riverside Church in New York, and known for his activism, especially in leading the opposition to the Vietnam War. These two respected each other greatly. William Sloane Coffin said, 'The trouble with your preaching, Billy, is that your Gospel never gets beyond the garden gate.' Like many Baptists, Billy Graham preached a gospel that was intensely personal and a gospel

---

1. Laurie Guy, 'JJ Doke—Baptists, Humanity and Justice' in David Bebbington & Martin Sutherland (eds), *Interfaces: Baptists and Others* (Milton Keynes UK: Paternoster Press, 2013), 265-91, 265.

that was domestic. This may have been the focus that enabled Billy Graham to have wide appeal but it left Baptists and other evangelicals impotent when it came to making a Christian impact in society. Laurie Guy says that the narrow 'conversionist model'[2] that hopes that changing individuals will have a 'trickle-down' effect and will make for a transformed society is commonly espoused by Baptists but it is inadequate. He calls 'half-converted' Baptists to be 'converted to humanity' as well as 'converted to Christ'.[3]

Charismatic leaders

Since their first baptisms in Sydney's Woolloomooloo Bay on Sunday 12 August 1832, Baptists in Australia have had periods when they have shown themselves to be very conscious of their social and political responsibilities.[4] Pastor of the Bathurst Street Baptist Church in Sydney, the Rev John Saunders (1806–1859), has been hailed as 'the most outstanding colonial Australian Baptist minister . . . and an exemplar of Christian social responsibility'.[5] The issues he championed in his time included temperance, aboriginal justice, the cause of British immigration and public education.

The life-size statue of Joseph H Goble (1863–1932) standing beside the Geelong Road in Footscray, Melbourne, is a tribute to this Baptist pastor of the Paisley Street Baptist Church (1895-1932)[6] who

---

2. Douglas Sturm, 'You Shall Have No Poor among You', in Michael G Long, *The Legacy of Billy Graham: Critical Reflections on America's Greatest Evangelist* (Louisville: Westminster John Knox Press, 2008), 63-77 at 63.
3. Guy, 'JJ Doke—Baptists, Humanity and Justice', 265.
4. Ken R Manley, *From Woolloomooloo to 'Eternity': A History of Australian Baptists. Volume 1: Growing an Australian Church (1831-1914)* (Milton Keynes, UK: Paternoster Press, 2006), 3.
5. Rod Benson, 'The Professional and Personal Witness of the Reverend John Saunders in Sydney, 1834-1847', *The Inaugural John Saunders Lecture*, 1 May 2008 at <http://www.baptisthistory.org.au/articles/00005.pdf>. Accessed 10 February 2014. More information on John Saunders can be found in Ken R. Manley & Michael Petras, *The First Australian Baptists* (Sydney: Baptist Historical Society of NSW, 1981), 53-64; Manley, *From Woolloomooloo to 'Eternity'*, 23-39, 41-43, 344f, 769f.
6. Monument Australia, 'Reverend Joseph Goble'. At <http://monumentaustralia.org.au/themes/people/religion/display/31327-reverend-joseph-goble> Accessed 10 February 2014.

championed the right of ordinary people to a decent standard of living, denounced the existence of unemployment as a national disgrace, and attacked the arms race and compulsory military training.[7]

In the second half of the twentieth century the Rev Dr Athol Gill (1937-1992) was a controversial fighter for justice.[8] The New Testament professor at Whitley College in Melbourne earthed his action in the Gospels and worked it out in conjunction with the Community Church of St Mark (Clifton Hill Baptist Church). Through his lectures, conference speaking and his books he inspired scores of Australians to be advocates for the poor and committed to the marginalised, the homeless and the 'little people'.[9]

In contemporary times, the Rev Tim Costello (1955-) has been one of Australia's leading voices on issues of social justice. As a Baptist minister in St Kilda and Collins Street he spearheaded public debates on prostitution, gambling, urban poverty, homelessness, reconciliation and substance abuse.[10] Now as CEO of World Vision Australia, Costello's focus has broadened to issues of global poverty and government aid.[11]

Through the years

From its beginnings in Australia, Baptist social and political action has generally been inspired by individuals such as John Saunders, Joseph Goble, Athol Gill and Tim Costello, rather than by denominational

---

7. John Lack, 'Goble, Joseph Hunter (1863-1932)', in *Australian Dictionary of Biography*, National Centre of Biography, Australian National University, <http://adb.anu.edu.au/biography/goble-joseph-hunter-6406/text10951> published in hardcopy 1983. Accessed 10 February 2014. This article was first published in hardcopy in *Australian Dictionary of Biography*, Volume 9, (Melbourne: Melbourne University Press), 1983.
8. Harold J Pidwell, *A Gentle Bunyip: The Athol Gill Story* (Adelaide: Seaview Press, 2007).
9. Books by Athol Gill include *The Fringes of Freedom: Following Jesus, Living Together, Working for Justice* (Sydney, NSW: Lancer Books, 1990); *Life on the Road: The Gospel Basis for a Messianic Lifestyle* (Sydney, NSW: Lancer Books, 1989; Scottdale, PA: Herald Press, 1992).
10. Tim Costello, *Streets of Hope: Finding God in St Kilda* (Melbourne: Albatross Books, 1998).
11. Tim Costello, *Hope: Moments of Inspiration in a Challenging World* (Melbourne: Hardie Grant Books, 2012).

task forces. Yet among Baptists, general social and political activism dwindled in the first few decades of the twentieth century. This disengagement with social issues, which sociologist David Moberg has called 'the great reversal', was not confined to Baptists or Australian evangelicals. It resulted from the impact of fundamentalism on the evangelical church throughout the world.[12] There came about a polarisation between evangelism and social concern. In this time when Christian mission was narrowed and 'social concerns dramatically disappeared or at least were subordinated to others', there was also a decline in any theologising that related to public life.[13] There was little thought about changing the structures of society and challenging people to find their vocation in public and political life. Where there was any social comment or political campaign, it was usually in the category of personal morality that frowned on such practices as drinking, smoking and gambling. Too often Baptists have defined themselves by what they are against, leaving it difficult for others to understand what they are standing for.

When early Baptists said 'No' to religious authority being vested in a church hierarchy based in Canterbury or Rome, they were saying 'Yes' to the Bible being the sole authority for all matters of belief and practice. While often this has meant a selective reading of Scripture, the strong commitment to the Bible does represent a hope that Baptists might embrace mission in all its breadth, including prayer and work towards seeing the Kingdom of God come on earth.

Thankfully, in recent decades, Baptist congregations are hearing not only about repentance and regeneration but also about reconciliation, refugees and racism. Churches formerly preoccupied with heaven and hell are now talking about housing. As well as espousing the doctrine of justification they are committing themselves to doing justice. They are still talking about evangelism but now they are becoming passionate about ecology. They major on prayer but they are getting fired up about poverty.[14]

---

12. David O Moberg, *The Great Reversal: Evangelism Versus Social Concern* (Philadelphia: J B Lippincott, 1972).
13. George M Marsden, *Fundamentalism and American Culture: The Shaping of Twentieth-century Evangelicalism, 1870-1925* (New York: Oxford University Press, 1980), 90.
14. This is adapted from 'Turning a Community Upside Down Through Worship and Ministry', in G Willis Bennett, *Effective Urban Church Ministry* (Nashville, TN: Broadman Press, 1983), 36.

Separation of Church and State

It is interesting that today we are meeting on the College Crescent or what used to be called the 'University Reserve'. Soon after the founding of the University of Melbourne in 1853 these 100 acres north of the main campus were allocated by the Victorian Parliament, and were set aside for residential colleges under the auspices of the churches.

The Roman Catholic Church was given the land on which Newman College was established. The Methodist Church accepted their ten acres, on which was established Queen's College and more recently St Hilda's. The Presbyterians were given the land on which Ormond was built. The Church of England was given their ten acres on which Trinity College was built and later the Janet Clarke Hall.

Land was offered to the Baptists but after a long, hard debate they declined the offer because of their historic commitment to the separation of church and state. Baptists have not always maintained such a clear position but they believed their prophetic edge would be blunted if they received land and monies from the government.[15]

Balancing autonomy and association

When Baptists rejected the authority of the state church and the church hierarchy, they were affirming the autonomy of each local congregation. There is no archbishop to acknowledge and no bishop to which Baptists must bow. Each local church with its Members' Meeting under God decides its life, practice and future.

Baptists have affirmed the importance of association with other churches and many voluntarily join with other Baptist churches in a 'Baptist Union' whereby they do together the work of such things as social service, theological training, ordination and international

---

15. It is interesting that the debate about receiving State aid was reopened in the 1950s which led to a modified stance and the establishment of Whitley College on Royal Parade, Parkville. 'The Annual Assembly of the Baptist Union [of Victoria] resolved in October 1954 "that the Church cannot preserve an attitude of complete separation from the State". Government assistance was acceptable provided That it would not compromise the freedom of the Church;
That it was equally open to other citizens or groups of citizens;
That it was for functions which are a Government responsibility but which the Government itself was unable to provide adequately.'
Roslyn Otzen, *Whitley: The Baptist College of Victoria 1891-1991* (Melbourne: Hyland House) 1991, 109.

mission. The state Baptist Union has little power over a local church while the Baptist Union of Australia and the Baptist World Alliance figure even less. This system of church government affects the degree to which Baptists get involved in the public sphere and the extent to which they get organised for addressing social and political issues.

Many voices

Who speaks for Baptists? This is a practical question in a grassroots movement but here is an example of the way it works. On 26 June 2012 the National President of Australian Baptist Ministries, the Rev Dr John Beasy, issued a public statement and letter to the then Prime Minister, saying that:

> Members of Baptist churches in Australia overwhelmingly support the current definition of marriage as between one man and one woman and reject moves to extend the definition to include same sex relationship... Australian Baptists strongly urge Prime Minister Julia Gillard, and politicians across the political spectrum to oppose moves to change the current legal definition of marriage by extending it to include same sex couples.[16]

The Rev Dr Simon Holt, Minister of the Collins Street Baptist Church in Melbourne, wrote on his blog shortly afterwards:

> I am a Baptist and I support gay marriage. I know that among Baptists I am in the minority on this issue. I also know this sets me apart from friends and colleagues I hold in high regard. But that's OK. Given our aversion to creeds, our adherence to freedom of conscience among believers, and our commitment to the autonomy

---

16. Australian Baptist Ministries, 'Australian Baptists View on Same Sex Marriage', 26/06/2012 at <http://www.baptist.org.au/News/Articles_and_Statements/Australian_Baptists_View_on_Same_Sex_Marriage.aspx>. Accessed 10 February 2014.

of the local church, we Baptists have room to differ. And we do. What troubles me is the energy with which some gatekeepers of Baptist life move to distance our denomination from people like me whenever our view is made public . . .

It feels to me as though we Baptists are afraid of the public perception that we hold a diversity of views on issues like this one . . .'[17]

Organising social action

How do Baptists organise themselves to make a difference in Australian society? The Baptist Union of Victoria has established a virtual network (called BEthos) of 'experts and working groups with people seconded, based on interest and expertise relevant to the issues being discussed.'[18] The working groups share and contribute to Baptist working groups in different states and countries as well as ecumenical taskforces.[19] The function of this network is to 'provide resources to support discussion, education, discernment and response to various public and social issues. Usually one issue is placed on the agenda for each Gathering of Victorian Baptists[20], often resulting in the passing of formal resolutions. In particular, this network and their papers help spokespersons such as the Director of Mission and Ministries, when responding to media questions or writing letters to the Australian government. A regular forum meets 'to brainstorm and workshop

---

17. Simon Carey Holt, Simply Simon, 'Baptists and Same-Sex Marriage', 14 May 2012 at <http://simoncareyholt.wordpress.com/2012/05/14/baptists-and-same-sex-marriage/> Accessed 10 February 2014.
18. Baptist Union of Victoria-Public Issues, 'Resourcing Churches and Leaders to respond to Public Issues: BEthos Virtual Network and Working Groups' at <http://www.buv.com.au/resource/public-issues>. Accessed 10 February 2014.
19. The website indicates collaboration with such groups as BapCare Australia, The Uniting Church of Australia, the Micah Challenge, Australian Religious Response to Climate Change (ARRCC) and the Victorian Inter-Church Gambling Taskforce.
20. The 'Gathering' is the term used for the former Baptist 'Assembly' meetings currently held twice a year, consisting of delegates elected by each local Baptist church that is formally connected to the Baptist Union of Victoria.

existing and emerging issues and provides focus and prioritisation for Working Groups.' Deciding on the social issues to address comes after considerable consultation with Baptists and more extensive consultations through regional forums around Victoria are planned in the future.[21]

The Victorian Baptist social agenda

What are the important matters in our current context for Victorian Baptists? The Baptist Union of Victoria currently provides papers and resources on these social issues:[22]

> Asylum Seekers with resolutions on asylum seekers generally (15 March 2002, October 2012), Children in Detention (5 December 2003) and letters to the Prime Minister seeking a compassionate and collaborative way forward (July 2013)
>
> Economic Justice including tax justice
>
> Environment including climate policy
>
> Gambling (with a resolution passed by Victorian Baptists in October 2013)
>
> Reconciliation in Australia
>
> Sexuality

The statement about sexuality illustrates the way Baptists in Victoria are currently handling the 'hot potato' issues when it says:

> The Baptist Union of Victoria continues to receive correspondence and pressure to articulate a clear

---

21. Nikki Capps, Head of Communications, Baptist Union of Victoria, Interview, 7 November 2013.
22. Baptist Union of Victoria-'Public Issues' at <http://www.buv.com.au/resource/public-issues>. Accessed 10 February 2014.

'Baptist' position on issues of homosexual practice, membership of churches [for gay people], and same sex marriage. But people in our churches hold very different views on these matters, in good faith. A top-down approach would be pre-emptive and ultimately unhelpful. The BUV's intent is to empower leaders to journey with their people into these discussions. Through the resources and opportunities provided, we want to help facilitate discussion and discernment within the church, characterised by great humility, tolerance and love. Instead of rushing to the familiar adversarial stances, we especially want people to consider missional and pastoral responses.[23]

Tolerance and tone in the public square

Baptists historically have been committed to the tenet of tolerance even if in practice such tolerance has not always been evident. This value means respecting the freedom and conscience of each individual to hold a certain position even if you disagree with their view. This is as much about tone as it is about content.

Australian theologian Gordon Preece states that 'one of the problems in much Christian public speaking is the attempt to be always prophetic, to thump the pulpit and speak in black and white tones.'[24] Do we speak into the public sphere in strident, categorical tones or do we pitch our statements in a more modest, open-ended style designed to evoke people's reflection and response? Is our stance condescending or do we value people as companions on a mutual quest?

Vision of the good life

Miroslav Volf, when writing about the modern multi-faith challenge, says:

---

23. Baptist Union of Victoria, 'Public Issues-Sexuality' at <http://www.buv.com.au/resource/public-issues/sexuality>. Accessed 10 February 2014.
24. Gordon Preece, 'Public speaking: Thick and Thin Theological Language and "Secular" Ethical Debate', *Ministry Society and Theology* 16 (2002): 26.

> When it comes to the public role of religions, the main fear is that of imposition—one faith imposing aspects of its own way of life on others. Religious people fear imposition—Muslims fear Christians, Christians fear Muslims, Jews fear both, Muslims fear Jews, Hindus fear Muslims, Christians fear Hindus and so on. Secularists, those who subscribe to no traditional religious faith at all, fear imposition as well—imposition by any faith—since they tend to deem all of them irrational and dangerous.[25]

The modern public square is like the hymn 'Where Cross the Crowded Ways'.[26] It is increasingly crowded and congested with numbers of faith ideas, some which share commonality and others that are in conflict. Into this maelstrom of fear and amid calls from those who think religion should stay out of politics, Volf argues that 'religious people ought to be free to bring their visions of the good life into the public sphere.'[27]

Another seeing

Amplifying this visionary role, Rowan Williams believes that one of the contributions that the public theologian brings to issues of concern is an 'imaginative awareness', 'another seeing', a 'different reading' of an issue—the ability to see things from fresh and constructive perspectives.[28]

The former Anglican Archbishop issues the challenge that we see ourselves as 'connecters'. Rowan Williams says doing public theology is a risky business and rather than offering a 'compendium of political theology', he offers his book, *Faith in the Public Square*, as 'a series of worked examples of trying to find the connecting points between

---

25. Miroslav Volf, A Public Faith: How Followers of Christ Should Serve the Common Good (Grand Rapids, MI: Brazos Press, 2011), x.
26. Hymn written by Frank Mason North in 1903. Words available at http://www.oremus.org/hymnal/w/w404.html. Accessed 10 February 2014.
27. Volf, *A Public Faith*, x.
28. Rowan Williams, *Faith in the Public Square* (London: Bloomsbury, 2012), 225.

various public questions and the fundamental beliefs about creation and salvation ... '

Integrated theology

About a decade ago, several Australian theologians repeated Martin Marty's call for a public church and a public theology.[29] A debate between Australian theologians Geoffrey Lilburne and Tony Kelly, largely conducted in the pages of the theological journal *Pacifica*, has focused on issues of methodology and the significance of the cultural context.[30] In the work of formulating an Australian theology, Lilburne calls theologians to a greater dialogue with 'the history and the culture of this place.'

Tony Kelly calls theologians and the community of faith not to ignore other communities in the public sphere such as the community of science and the community of art. Bringing theology together with other disciplines such as ecology and cosmology, he contends, will make for a more integrated theology and is 'a move to put our souls back into our bodies.'[31]

Conversation in the public sphere

When much of the discussion of public theology was centering on issues of methodology, Frank Rees sought to overcome the stalemate with an article presenting a 'conversational' alternative.[32] He offers some starters for an Australian theological discussion and concludes by expressing the hope for some 'collaborative conversational explorations through which an Australian theology might produce such fruit.' This conversational approach by Rees is both positive and refreshing because it highlights the hope that theology and

---

29. Martin Marty, *The Public Church* (New York: Crossroad Publishing, 1981).
30. While *Pacifica* is not the only place where these two scholars have presented their views on an Australian theology, Geoffrey Lilburne's contribution in this journal is called 'Contextualising Australian Theology: An Enquiry into Method', *Pacifica* 10 (1997): 350-364 and Tony Kelly's article, 'Whither "Australian Theology"? A Response to Geoffrey Lilburne', *Pacifica* 12 (1999): 192-208.
31. Tony Kelly, *An Expanding Theology: Faith in a World of Connections* (Sydney: E J Dwyer, 1993), 12-14.
32. Frank Rees, 'Beating around the Bush: Methodological Directions for Australian Theology', *Pacifica* 15 (2002), 293.

public discourse be essentially a shared activity. Public theology as conversation has the capacity to develop a culture of courtesy and respect, which is all too lacking in the public arena. The proposals offered by Rees, that these explorations discuss the questions about identity, community, belonging, freedom, responsibility, worth and destiny in the Australian context, are useful suggestions for the direction of a shared conversation and a public theology in Australia.

Training in social policy

In many Australian theological Colleges and seminaries around the world it has been heartening to see sprouting up some centres of public theology and institutes for religion and social policy.[33] These coalitions are heeding this call, offering specific training in this field and providing resources to offer a strong theological grounding and help people make meaningful connections between their faith and the issues they are confronting in society.

By all means

Baptists might be known for their diverse viewpoints about religious and social policy but it would be good to encourage diversity when it comes to the means by which our views are expressed. In the Baptist tradition social commentators have historically done it through sermons, public lectures, brochures and tracts. The Victorian Baptist minister, Dr FW Boreham, wrote more than 3,000 newspaper editorials over forty-seven years in the pages of the Hobart *Mercury*, the Melbourne *Age* and the *Argus*. The Rev Tim Costello regularly expresses his views in succinct sound bytes appropriate to television audiences. Michael Leunig has expressed his social and political views through his cartoons and poems. Missiology professor, Dr Ross Langmead (1949-2013), has made an important contribution to

---

33. These include the Australian Centre for Christianity and Culture at Charles Sturt University, Canberra; the St Mark's National Theological Centre (Anglican) in Canberra;, the United Theological College (Uniting Church in Australia) in Sydney; the Tinsley Institute, Morling College (Baptist), Sydney; and the Yarra Institute for Religion and Social Policy (Ecumenical), Melbourne.

awakening people to the needs in society through his many songs.[34] On the wall outside the St Michael's Catholic church and school in Ashburton, students have painted a colourful mural featuring Australians of different appearance, culture and religion. It bears the words: 'We all belong!'

Whether our medium is words, images, songs, acting or marching, whether our platforms are pulpits, stages, newspapers, graffiti, television and radio programmes, blogs, YouTube videos, Facebook updates or Twitter tweets, we have an abundance of creative possibilities whereby as Christians we can express our hopes for Australia and thus make a vital difference.

---

34. Many of the songs of Ross Langmead (1949-2013) can be found at <http://rosslangmead.50webs.com/rl/songs.html>. Accessed 10 February 2014. They are also published in Ross Langmead, *On the Road: Sixteen Songs for the Christian Community to Sing* (Melbourne: Ross Langmead, 1987).

Anglican Social Thinking for Australia: Making a Difference?

Ray L Cleary

The claim of the Christian Church to make its voice heard in matters of politics and economics is widely resented, even by those who are Christian in personal belief and in devoted practice.[1]

William Temple wrote those words in November 1941 when Archbishop of Canterbury and when the Church of England was central to public life in the United Kingdom. They were spoken at a time when the Church of England, as the Established Church, was actively involved in influencing and shaping much of British civil society with the bishop and local vicar respected and embedded in community life. The Anglican Church in Australia, although not an established church, has played a similar role in the public domain until more recent times, but admittedly not to the same extent as in the United Kingdom. Temple's words still resonate today in many parts of Western Society, including Australia, in comments on social, economic, moral and political issues by Christian and other leaders, while at the same time the authority of the church and the legitimacy of religion to influence civil society have come under increasing scrutiny and challenge.

In Australia today, journalists, academics, writers of opinion pieces, along with increasing numbers of community members, see the Christian message and the church as relics of a past era, speaking on matters from an historical and ethical perspective that has little if

---

1. William Temple, *Christianity and Social Order* (London: Pelican Books, 1941), 5.

any relevance to the present. The claim is often made that in many areas of ethics the church's influence has restricted personal liberty and caused a great deal of hurt and pain, particularly in the area of personal morality. Others such as the late Christopher Hitchens and Richard Dawkins, representative of a range of concerned citizens, see religion and belief in God as the cause of much evil in today's world, inflicting on many people guilt and bondage, limiting creativity and stifling open debate on matters of human sexuality, rights, freedom and pleasure.[2] Religion is seen as naïve belief leading to terror and destruction. The church has not responded well to these challenges and criticisms, often appearing to ignore them and resisting constructive dialogue.

At the same time, and from my personal perspective, leadership in the church has not always been exercised with tolerance, with consistent attacks on those who fail to live up to or accept the moral teachings of the Church. There is a failure to listen. David Hall explains it this way:

> The threats of which I am thinking include not only terrorism and counter terrorism, but economic injustice and the misdistribution of global resources, environmental degradation, the oppression of women and children, global encircling diseases, and the many other impediments to creaturely well being that use and misuse the religious impulse for their inspiration. The day is over when 'religion' could be thought of as an unambiguously Good Thing, as many in the past believed it to be. Informed and sensitive members of every faith tradition today are likely to think twice, if not explicitly to demur, when they hear themselves described as a 'religious person.'[3]

---

2. Richard Dawkins and Christopher Hitchens are two writers who advocate the rejection of religion. For further discussion, see Richard Dawkins, *The God Delusion* (New York: Mariner Books, 2008); Christopher Hitchens, *God is not Great* (New York: Hatchette Book Group, 2007).
3. David Hall, *Waiting for Gospel, An Appeal to the Dispirited Remnants of Protestant "Establishment"* (Eugene, OR: Cascade Books, 2012), 160.

I recall Philip Ruddock, when he was Minister for Immigration in the mid-1990s, saying similar things when he criticised leaders of faith-based agencies in Melbourne. In a discussion about boat people, asylum seekers and refugees, he chastised the gathered leaders of these organisations, telling them that if it were not for the churches and their agencies there would be no debate on the government's policies towards asylum seekers. The rest of the nation was not interested or concerned. Similarly, Alexander Downer, then Foreign Minister, on one occasion described clerics as seekers of 'cheap headlines' and who

> . . . are remarkably vague and uncertain about matters which their faith should teach them with certitude, but remarkably certain and dogmatic on matters of considerable complexity and ambiguity about which they have no practical experience.[4]

Further, a leading economist, when challenged about free market economics during a forum sponsored by church agencies when the GST was being proposed in the early 1990s, responded that the agencies need not worry, as their job and the agencies themselves were safe. He saw that the agencies' role was to pick up the fall-out from the 'market'. The examples quoted suggest strongly that the once powerful voice of the church on social and economic issues in Australia is now disputed, not only for what the church says, but also for what it represents.

Noting the above challenges is not to suggest that the church should have privilege or be immune from criticism, nor do we have, as Archbishop Desmond Tutu says in his book, *God is not a Christian: Speaking the Truth in a Time of Crisis*, a monopoly over morality.[5] Morality has been seen to be lacking in the church itself in recent times and its previous moral authority weakened and insufficient today to address the social and economic issues challenging our

---

4. Quoted in Raymond L Cleary, 'The Church and Civil Society: Mission Imperatives', *Church and Civil Society*, edited by Francis Sullivan and Sue Leppert (Adelaide: ATF Press, 2004). 116.
5. Desmond Tutu, *God is not a Christian: Speaking the Truth in a Time of Crisis* (London: Rider, 2011). The book has a fuller discussion on Christian morality.

nation. Substance in discussion and debate is often absent. The churches, including many of the agencies associated with the church, know they have failed on many occasions and have been corrupted and seduced by power and privilege, often unintentionally. Robert Fitzgerald, then president of the Australian Council of Social Services (ACOSS), speaking at a Melbourne City Mission staff symposium in the late 1990s, asked whom the community sector was supporting. Was it government, itself or the poor? It is the same question we must continue to ask of faith-based agencies, as they appear to rush into more contracts and grow ever larger. The ecumenical spirit of the 1960s to the 1980s appears to be over and co-operation replaced by competition.

The church in Australia has a long and active engagement with Australian society, a role understood in earlier times as proper and legitimate in the public domain. There were many synergies between church and state on matters of personal morality, the family and the role of government. Today the church is in a different context, often muted and ignored for a perceived lack of integrity, transparency and failures in its own life. The mission of the church has been compromised and its credibility tarnished. The welfare and justice agencies of the churches grow larger and their voices as faith-based organisations are, in some cases, increasingly marginalised from their own tradition, and muted on matters of justice.[6]

I am not a cradle Anglican, nor did I attend an Anglican or any church-sponsored school. My parents could not support the fees, nor as civic Christians did they see any point in doing so. I did attend a major state secondary school where the pursuit of academic achievement and sport were the highest goals. Religion was discouraged, often in a hostile manner, by many of the staff except for the thirty-minute religious education assembly each month. These assemblies were also often a great embarrassment and there was no commitment to them by the school principal or staff. From my mid-teens, however, I did attend an Anglican catholic parish where social justice, outreach to the community and beautiful worship went hand in hand. My introduction to justice was not so much from the pulpit

---

6. Raymond Cleary, *Reclaiming Welfare for Mission, Choices for Churches* (Canberra: Barton Books, 2012). The book details the relationship between agencies and their faith tradition.

or church teaching as by the actions of individuals. This is often still the case. Listening to the stories of others can be both profoundly moving and challenging. Local people engaged in voluntary work as part of their Christian commitment and speakers who came and preached on Sundays introduced me to the agencies of the church and their work among the poor.[7] This was common in Anglican circles at the time. Initiatives to engage the poor and care for the homeless were driven not by any central church or diocesan command, but by parishes and individuals. These initiatives led to the establishment of the agencies of today, such as Anglicare and the Brotherhood of St Laurence, many of which were originally parish outreach programs. Many of the early philanthropists had a strong sense of Christian duty and established and funded the work of charity from their own resources and without the support of their governing body. Even now a fine line is often present in defining the relationship between the agencies of the Anglican Church and the diocesan authorities. In many places evangelism is seen as the primary Christian agenda, with justice and service to others a secondary concern.

Today, in the post-modern (or is it now the post-modern and post-secular?) context in which we find ourselves, churches and religion in general no longer have regular and automatic access to media. Regular attempts are made to marginalise the Christian narrative. Serious religious discussion is curtailed and often only the trivial and sensational given a voice. Religion is increasingly presented as comedy and entertainment. The exception is the increasing role of social media in providing an emerging platform for faith comment and discussion. The present approach by mainstream media can be seen in the selective reporting on matters pertaining to belief and faith, often looking for the eccentric, the outrageous and the provocative voice. Religious reporting often lacks objective analysis and lacks historical knowledge. The partnership between the State and religious institutions is often ignored in discussions about the failures of institutional care and society's attitude is out of sight, out of mind. While the role of church agencies in failing to protect children cannot be ignored, the State, the police and the law were also complicit.

---

7. Speakers and preachers, from agencies such as the Brotherhood of St Laurence, regularly visited the local Anglican parish I attended in the 1960s.

The privileged place of Christianity as the faith of the nation is now seen as one among many narratives that seek to shape and influence our multi-cultural, multi-faith and multi-ethnic nation. In the minds and attitudes of many, including journalists, the Gospel parables of the Good Samaritan and the Prodigal Son, along with the Sermon on the Mount, are increasingly distant stories about our responsibility to others, the divine presence and the call to justice. Many Australians no longer recognise a connection with the Christian understanding of justice and compassion as core values. Nor do they know the source of such values. At the same time, the historical influence the churches have had on the shape, values and direction of Australian society is rarely spoken about with any rigorous assessment, and many times seems foreign to the journalist's own experience and interest. This may simply be because we no longer teach history and journalists are often ignorant of the historical place of religion.

The church can no longer assume that the Christian narrative, as recorded in the Gospels and interpreted in the life of the Christian community, alongside biblical interpretation and the context of the times, is valued as in the past. We are therefore at a new place in history and previous assumptions are no longer relevant. The Christian understanding of sin, all that separates us from God, has been lost on most of Australian society and is no longer accepted as the standard for moral and ethical behaviour. This is not to say that the church has always got it right or that mistakes have not been made. A brief reading of history will confirm otherwise, in particular the church's attitudes to sexuality, the role of women, human rights and the care of the poor. Research, theological reflection and experience tell us that Christian faith has not always liberated people from bondage, but rather the reverse. Father has not always known best and still appears to struggle in many quarters.

What I have outlined is an attempt to explain why the church's influence has waned, and if faith and belief are secondary, the broader question is why as a nation does our commitment to care for our neighbour also appear to be floundering? Denial and self-interest alongside erratic political behaviour have become what is to be expected. Have the past twenty-five years of rapid free market economics, with the emphasis on self, permeated our values and identity to such an extent that we cannot see beyond the immediate and the self?

This leads me to suggest at this point that traditional approaches by the churches in speaking into the public forum need to be rethought and new ways explored. Commenting on every social and economic evil of the day with a press statement only saturates the market and leads to desensitisation. Choosing when to speak is important in ensuring the message is heard. It is also important to recognise that solutions to issues are not always likely to be unanimous. The big picture and the highest of hopes need to be addressed more rigorously, and at times our best contribution may be to moderate or facilitate discussion.

Rowan Williams, in his 2013 book, *Faith in the Public Square*, argues strongly for a renewed engagement by the church with society. He says: 'The Christian faith is not a matter of vague philosophy, but of unremitting challenge to what we think we know about human beings and their destiny.'[8] Williams' comments affirm that the Christian faith does have something profound to say about the human condition and, I would add, the immediate predicament the church finds itself in. It is first to acknowledge that the Christian church is no longer *the* stakeholder, but *a* stakeholder in seeking to win the hearts and minds of people. The challenge, first and foremost, is to examine ourselves if we are to speak into the culture of the day. It is more likely, I suggest, that when we address our own failures as church our witness will be enhanced and the Christian narrative will be taken more seriously.

Brian Trainor, in his recent book, *Sacred Precedes Secular: Why the State Needs the Church*, speaks in a similar vein when he argues for a more active and decisive engagement of faith with the secular state.[9] The task here is to adjudicate or mediate between the various cultural and religious traditions, to seek the common threads for the building of a more just society. Like Williams and Miroslav Volf, Trainor opposes the growing view that the future should be determined by the human race alone and without any influence of religious belief.[10]

For Christians, the ethic of God's purpose for the creation exemplified in the life, death, ministry and resurrection of Jesus

---

8. Rowan Williams, *Faith in the Public Square* (London: Bloomsbury Publishing, 2012), 1.
9. Brian Trainor, *Sacred Precedes Secular: Why the State Needs the Church* (Melbourne: Mosaic Press, 2013), 5.
10. Trainor, *Sacred Precedes Secular*, 5ff.

provides a solid and vibrant code for relationships and belonging, central to understanding what it means to be human. Speaking and participating in the public sphere is mission. It is mission to the world. At the heart of mission is wisdom, wisdom that St Paul reminds us is folly to the world, but stronger and wiser than all human endeavours. Wisdom is not to be understood only as acquired knowledge, but rather how we are called to live our lives in relationship to the whole of the created order. It is wisdom of the highest order, embracing all that is noble, self-sacrificing and devoid of self, that the church has to offer to a broken and complex world. It is wisdom expressed in our relationships and service to the other, as Christ served the world, wisdom that is not based on power, but on mutual trust and dialogue. Wisdom is the fullness of what it means to be human, created in God's image. Wisdom, God's wisdom, is the recognition of loss, of not knowing mystery, awe and transcendence, beyond the self. It is also a reminder to us not to confuse morality with wisdom.

The church's participation in the public sphere should be more than short-lived comments from religious leaders on social and economic matters, to name just two responses, but must be lived in its own life and the life of those agencies and organisations that claim affiliation. Put simply, we must practise what we preach. Wisdom speaks divine love and God's dream for the created order that embraces all that is just, expressed in our deepest concerns for each other and for God. The words spoken must offer opportunities for personal and social transformation and the recognition of the divine presence in all of life. Miroslav Volf speaks about this idea when he says:

> Christian faith is therefore a prophetic faith that seeks to mend the world ... Faith should be active in all spheres of life: education and the arts, business and politics, communication and entertainment and more.[11]

One practical expression of acting differently from others could be in the way we treat staff and employees in our agencies or in the corporate life of the churches.

Is the Church's relevance today a response only to our own behaviour? Have we been too pre-occupied with ourselves, ignoring

---

11. Miroslav Volf, *A Public Faith* (Grand Rapids, MO: Brazos Press, 2011), xv.

the cries of others, or is the Christian call so radical to the empires of today, and the antithesis to power and corruption, that the challenges facing us are overwhelming? Our bias for the poor and oppressed, however, as Henri Nouwen says, is where the voice of the crucified one will be heard and faith restored:

> Those who are marginal in the world are central in the Church, and that is how it is supposed to be! Thus we are called as members of the Church to keep going to the margins of our society. The homeless, the starving, parentless children, people with AIDS, our emotionally disturbed brothers and sisters–they require our first attention.
>
> We can trust that when we reach out with all our energy to the margins of our society we will discover that petty disagreements, fruitless debates, and paralysing rivalries will recede and gradually vanish. The Church will always be renewed when our attention shifts from ourselves to those who need our care. The blessing of Jesus always comes to us through the poor. The most remarkable experience of those who work with the poor is that, in the end, the poor give more than they receive. They give food to us.[12]

In contrast to the absolute statements made by those who claim leadership in the church today, Jesus rarely gave a straight or expected answer to a question. His response to the religious and political leaders in the context of the day defied logic and rationality in their eyes. It challenged their understanding of God's identity and purposes and made them feel uncomfortable. While they frowned, the crowds followed. David Hall, writing on the church's decline in influencing the western world, claims that the dumbing down of faith into simplistic jargon and packaging has contributed significantly to the decline. He says:

---

12. Henri JM Nouwen, *Bread for the Journey: A Daybook of Wisdom and Faith* (San Francisco: Harper, 1997).

> Christianity, as faith centered in Jesus, as the Christ came to be called, got a foothold in the world, and a vital and vocal minority changed the world, because it proclaimed a message that awakened men and women to possibilities for human life that they either lost or never entertained.[13]

He goes on to say that the established churches 'are prevented from proclaiming gospel precisely on account of their establishment, or the remnants of the same.'[14] This coupled with the shift in meaning of language and style has largely contributed to the decline. In effect we have dumbed down the Christian message to slick words often lacking depth and exposing ourselves to ridicule and challenge. At the same time, when we say church what do we mean? How do we reconcile the voice of those who sell religion as a sign of God's providence and promote prosperity as an outcome of belief? Compassion for the poor and justice for all is a sideline activity.

The reality of loss, the loss of influence and the place of Christendom are, however, only barely acknowledged by many in the mainstream churches. We have been 'seduced by the spoils' and, like other previously respected and even revered institutions, have accepted many aspects of the prevailing empire. One of the most critical issues, then, to be faced in re-establishing a prophetic calling is to begin with the church itself and review how it engages with the wider community and its own governance and decision-making. The first task then is to speak to the church, to seek to regain a credible voice in the market place of ideas and to build bridges between the agencies of the church. This needs to involve a commitment to renewed ecumenism and stronger connections with the social justice arms of the churches appropriate for our times, so that we can speak together as often as we are able. The loss of a strong ecumenical voice by the National Council of Churches and local state bodies has helped marginalise the broad church response and allowed the Australian Christian Lobby to fill a vacuum. How are we to be a moderating influence in debates on social and economic issues within our churches and with the wider community, including our political leaders? How does one address the one-minute grab?

---

13. Hall, *Waiting for Gospel*, xi.
14. Hall, *Waiting for Gospel*, xv.

This challenge also recognises that, despite the context in which the church finds itself, it is not the same as saying that religion and faith are irrelevant to the modern world. Rather it is, as I said earlier, the challenge to find new ways of speaking not as *the* stakeholder, but as *one* of the stakeholders in the dialogue. During my time as the leader of Anglicare, I constantly asked staff to explain to me what difference a faith perspective brought to the table in social policy. I am not suggesting in asking this question that people with faith and those without faith do not have anything in common. Anglicanism by its nature is diverse and fragmented. Our national church lacks power and influence across the dioceses. There is a shortage of resources within the national body, yet wealth in our agencies. This is a matter I think all of us who speak for the church need to give more attention to at this time.

Many of us, those who exercise leadership in faith-based agencies or commissions, are regular commentators and voices for the Church, but are our comments reflective of a faith understanding that frames and influences our response to issues? Are we just expressing views that sound too often like a repeat of our secular brothers and sisters or those of another faith? I regularly read comments made by church spokespeople and conclude that what they have to say is good, but not necessarily reflective of faith. Have we been so seduced or are we so fearful of using language and imagery that challenges the emptiness and devaluing of so many people that we now avoid it? Passion and belief in the capacity of the Gospel to challenge our commitment to ideology that reflects self-interest and not compassion require taking risks and challenging the power of the empire.

How then does our mission assist the fulfillment of the two great commissions to be found in the gospels of Matthew and Luke? The Anglican tradition, unlike the Roman Catholic Church, does not have a codified set of laws, dogma or teaching clearly setting out policies and principles. This is in part due to the nature of the Anglican Communion and reflects its diversity and lack of a central magisterium. Anglican polity and governance is decentralised with the primary authority being the local bishop in Synod. This is not to say that there is no social teaching, only that it is likely to vary across dioceses, despite consisting of principles and values that reflect an understanding of what it means to be created in the image of God.

This image is reflected in the person of Jesus in his ministry expressing the human face of God's love and compassion for all people. It is also likely to be general, drawing on principles, and not specific, other than motions passed by Synods. I might add, often with minimal debate. Anglicans may agree that poverty should be eradicated, but will have different views on how this should be achieved.

Some would argue that Britain as a colonial power articulated a social and political agenda of subservience and exploitation in the name of the Christian God during its time of imperial expansion and domination. Church of England missionaries accompanied the soldiers. While truth may be found in this understanding of the growth of the worldwide Anglican communion, there were many other countries of other religious traditions that did the same. What may, however, be considered as a form of social teaching for Anglicans, at least over the past 150 years, can be traced to the cleric FD Maurice and the Christian Socialist movement in the United Kingdom in the mid-nineteenth century. It should be noted, however, that his approach to social issues was often seen as pragmatic, a vehicle to achieve certain goals, rather than theological or ideological. Maurice was not a social revolutionary, but rather believed that a new order would rise in which the labouring classes would take their place in reasserting the foundations of society as seen in the ministry, life, death and resurrection of Jesus. Consistent principles, however, were hard to find. Like others of his time, Maurice differed in his approach to specific issues, self-help on the one hand and government intervention on the other.

Perhaps similar approaches can be seen today. Alan Wilkinson claims that Maurice and others who were the leaders of the Christian Socialist movement of the times arose as a response to possible revolution, poverty and inequality.[15] These early stirrings saw others such as Henry Scott Holland and Charles Gore in the 1880s come to the fore. The twentieth century saw William Temple, influential in the post-war Welfare State in Britain, followed by a variety of supporters working in the East End of London, including Kenneth Leech and David Hope. In Australia, Bishop Ernest Burgmann in Canberra, known as the 'Red Bishop' and described by many as standing in

---

15. Alan Wilkinson, *Christian Socialism: Scott Holland to Tony Blair* (London: SCM Press, 1998).

the tradition of Maurice, and others expressed strong views about privilege and justice.[16]

Anglicans, since the time of the First Fleet, have played an active and significant role in working with and among some of the most disadvantaged and excluded people in the Australian community, first as chaplains and moral exponents of the Christian faith to prisoners, soldiers and free settlers of the first settlements. Those imprisoned had been separated from family and friends when transported to Australia, many for petty crimes. The prisoners themselves were victims of poverty and duress. In sentencing men, women and children, little attention was given to their living conditions or wellbeing.

At the international level, Archbishop Desmond Tutu, for over forty years following the leadership of Trevor Huddleston, has been a tireless exponent of a Christian understanding of justice, challenging both the churches and the global community. Not only was he an outspoken critic of apartheid in South Africa, but he still is everywhere that injustice exists and people are exploited. In recent days, a new approach to addressing global issues, internal church divisions and how to use the media in a constructive way has been demonstrated by Justin Welby, Archbishop of Canterbury, and Pope Francis. Both speak with a sense of humility and openness to dialogue and engagement with others. They bring a fresh voice to a range of issues, including global economics and greed, sexuality and human rights. Their approach is less dogmatic and more pastoral and conciliatory.

In 1937, Bishop Burgmann stirred the conscience of the Australian nation and his brother bishops in the then Church of England in Australia, when he spoke about his dream for a great Australian nation:

> There is one way and one way only to save the drift and that is by giving the people of Australia a vision of the Christian faith recreating the social order in this new land; leaving behind the bitterness of the old world with its class hatreds and its international rivalries;

---

16. For a discussion of Bishop Burgmann, see Peter Hempenstall, 'An Anglican Strategy for Social Responsibility', in *Anglican Strategies from Burgmann to the Present*, (Brisbane: Broughton Press, 1989).

> establishing justice in economic fields and inspiring political action to great creative endeavours. The Christian faith did this once for Europe when it tamed barbarians and sustained a vision of unity for the whole continent. The Christian faith is still as vital and as relevant as it ever was or is to Europe, but the churches must forget most of the things, which now obsess them, and be caught by a vision of the work to be done.[17]

As noted earlier, the commitment to justice by Anglicans in Australia has been defined by a set of broad Christian principles and by theological engagement in issues. The approach has relied upon the insights and the commitment of individuals who braved the 'established' nature of the Church of England in Australia, as it was known until 1962.[18] Burgmann was scathing of the establishment nature of the church of his time:

> It is the business of the Church to minister to sick and neurotic souls [yet] it ends up far too often, with these fearful, neurotic souls in the saddle so far as the institution is concerned... The Church has failed to bear witness to international justice as she has failed to bear witness to justice in inter-class relations. As her failure in the latter case produced communism, so her failure in the former has given us Nazism and fascism... Churches are always a danger to religion. They get interested in themselves, in their own in-ground aggrandisement and power, and countless things that keep them too busy to live closely to the life of the people. .... Churchmen get interested in the world beyond this world, largely to escape the trouble [of] setting right the wrongs that afflict the human race.[19]

Others who followed in his footsteps included Sister Esther of the Community of the Holy Name, Father Tucker of the Brotherhood of

---

17. Hempenstall, *Anglican Strategies*, 2.
18. Hempenstall, *Anglican Strategies*, 4.
19. Hempenstall, *Anglican Strategies*, 5.

St Laurence, Bishop Geoffrey Sambell and Sister Kate. In more recent times, the voice of Anglicare Australia, the peak body for Anglican justice and welfare providers, speaks with the same passion and voice. Central to all the names I have noted, both in Australia and abroad, is that they all based their theological understanding of what it means to be human on the 'word made flesh', with the Church's task to spell out and implement God's deep passion for the creation, the kingdom of God (Isaiah 61:1-2; Luke 4:18-19), a kingdom or community where God is sovereign and where people are created in the image of God, as one who is compassionate, forgiving, merciful and generous. At the centre of this understanding is our relationship with God, with one another and with the whole of the created order. Time does not permit us to discuss that there were those within the Church of England at the time of Maurice who were dismayed and alarmed at what Maurice and his contemporaries were doing,[20] believing more strongly in social inequality as divinely ordained. One had to accept one's place in life:

> So long as the working man maintained order and decorum, and kept the peace and observed the law of the land, and was a respectable member of the community, so long he felt satisfied the working man would meet with the sympathy and approval of those in order of providence who were placed in a higher and another position in life.[21]

William Temple sought to respond to the criticism of the times, of this emerging and prevailing social comment by church leaders, by emphasising that Christians should exercise their moral responsibilities in a Christ-like spirit, exercise their civil rights in a Christian spirit, and critique those who offended Christian principles. He went on to say that the Church should not always offer solutions to the problems, but should raise the level of debate.[22]

In Australia, it has been Anglican agencies that have been the regular and constant advocates on matters of justice in recent years.

---

20. See Wilkinson, *Christian Socialism*, chapters 2-6, for a detailed discussion.
21. Temple, *Christianity and Social Order*, 14.
22. Temple, *Christianity and Social Order*, 16.

On occasion, archbishops have spoken on such matters as gambling, foreign aid, asylum seekers and similar matters, but it has been the agencies and a small number of prophetic and socially active parishes that have borne the responsibilty for social comment, advocacy and action. Social Responsibility Committees and the Public Affairs Committee of General Synod have been the other source of public comment, but in recent years most have been starved of funds and bishops often appear reluctant to use the advice of the committees or the resources of the agencies. A shared voice on matters of justice and shared leadership with the agencies appear at times to be fragmented and often lacking coordination. This approach also reflects the fragile structure of the Anglican Church of Australia.

A distinctive Christian and Anglican response to the social, economic and ethical issues facing Australia today and in the future will require a more robust and rigorous attention to detail, and a vision that goes beyond the immediate to future generations. It should involve a declaration of intent that justice is integral to the church's mission, and not an optional extra. It should express the view that to be fully human is not about happiness and the acquisition of goods and services, but a recognition that life is more than an accident and that creation has a purpose other than self. Mission, the church's mission, embraces a justice perspective that calls us into relationships, with the Divine and each other. This is not simply an Anglican viewpoint, but a common thread running through other faith traditions too. Speaking into the public forum is mission, a commitment to reflect Christ's mission to the world, a mission that is vigorous, vibrant and prophetic. As Rowan Williams says, how do we recover a sense of 'convergent belief in the possibility of liberation from the systems of violent struggle, in a way that genuinely opens doors in our world'?[23]

The world in which we live is complex, challenging and increasingly interconnected. The Global Financial Crisis of 2008 clearly demonstrated the extent to which we are all part of a global economy where the rules appear to be increasingly set, not by national governments, but by powerful lobby groups concerned with their own interests. The world we live in is complex and contested, with differing ideologies, religions and understandings of the role of government in shaping and influencing the machinery of

---

23. Williams, *Faith in the Public Square*, 303.

government and equally of individuals. I repeat: this is a contested world of ideologies, religions, and viewpoints, all seeking to win the hearts and minds of their constituents. Central to each are issues that directly affect the planet's future, our future, the next generation's future and whether we can live in harmony with one another and the planet. Economics, human rights, multi-faith communities, the role and makeup of families, the environment, the distribution of wealth, and sexuality are some of the issues that are currently hotly debated in both the global and the Australian community. The response of the Church to these issues is critical not only as part of a healthy civil society, but because the Church has something profound to offer. The response, however, must be more than five-second sound grabs and sets of absolute rules, and must not be left to the fundamentalists or the self-proclaimed moral authority of sects.

In his most recent book on the church's engagement in an increasingly secular or humanist society on matters of economics and social order, Rowan Williams says that:

> The Church is . . . the trustee of a vision that is radical and universal, the vision of a social order that is without fear, oppression, the violence of exclusion and the search for scapegoats because it is one where each recognises their dependence on all and each is seen as having an irreplaceable gift for all.[24]

In arguing for a robust, prophetic and visionary faith, that acknowledges how the church itself has been seduced and sedated by its own power and privileged position, Williams further argues for a lesser emphasis on matters of sexuality, gender roles and family. Present debates around issues of human sexuality, gender and family are unlikely to gain consensus in the near future. He acknowledges how on these matters the church has pursued a narrow moral agenda and a lack of interest in many other areas, such as population control, climate change and relationships.

Given the diversity of the Anglican Church in Australia, it is unlikely that consensus on all issues will be possible, nor may this be

---

24. Williams, *Faith in the Public Square*, 305.

desirable. As a minimum, a vision of ministry and engagement with Australian society should include the following:

- An understanding that the sacred and the divine are grounded in our very being, both as individuals and the wider creation;
- A commitment to love and service to others as core Christian teaching, exemplified in the Sermon on the Mount and the parables of Jesus;
- A recognition and affirmation that agencies and parishes are called to make a real difference to the lives of individuals and the communities in which they are located;
- A commitment to the value of research and community living alongside scripture and the traditions of the Church;
- A willingness to take risks and to acknowledge that our own salvation is diminished when we fail to heed the cry of the other;
- A preparedness to listen to the voice of the faithful and those without Christian faith as they journey through life;
- A willingness to share leadership on matters of justice with like-minded individuals and organisations;
- A recognition that good works, charity and benevolence, while admirable in their intent, are symptoms of disadvantage and brokenness. Challenging the structures of society that limit, diminish or exploit requires perseverance and advocacy;
- A willingness to share the pain and the brokenness of the world, acknowledging the presence of the Divine in the midst of human suffering;
- A willingness to be open to the disturbing spirit of God in the Church's own life and in the community.

The challenges and immediate issues

I have already outlined the first challenge. It is the challenge to the church to rethink and respond to the current context with greater integrity and to acknowledge the part the church has played in the formation of our present society. On matters of justice, governance, transparency, and prophetic teaching, we need to speak to ourselves as well as to the wider community. The churches collectively in

Australia are one of the largest employers in the country, if not the largest. Through its network of schools, colleges, universities, welfare agencies, hospitals and parishes, it employs many thousands of people from diverse backgrounds. How do we model best employment practice, given our role and responsibility? How do we safeguard or reconcile family life with our work practices? Why do we continue to discriminate against those with whom Jesus himself would have connected and engaged? Are our governance structures open and accountable? Other issues the church needs to address include population growth, human sexuality, and climate change. There is the need, as Walter Brueggemann says in his latest book, *The Practice of Prophetic Imagination: Preaching an Emancipating Word*, to re-engage and to redefine our role as a participant in public discussion as one among many and without privilege. Do we live, as church and as Christians, the vision of radical discipleship, of a society without fear and abuse? While recognising there is no single way to respond to culture, Brueggemann identifies the following as a way forward:

1. The need to take the present seriously and acknowledge our part in creating the present;
2. The need to identify the causes of the present challenges facing the community and to name them publicly;
3. The need to accept that we may not be able to reverse trends in either the short or long term;
4. The need to recognise our own loss of identity and acceptance;
5. The need to immerse ourselves in the issues of the day and to equip ourselves with data and information for action, valuating the options.[25]

He goes on to say that central to all these issues is the need to reclaim our passion for God and a voice to lead into a new realm where how we relate to one another and to God becomes the core business of mission. This will involve a greater willingness to partner with others and to acknowledge that, although we are not the only stakeholder, we are not a community of self-interest seeking privilege, but a community meeting needs.

---

25. Walter Brueggemann, *The Practice of Prophetic Imagination: Preaching an Emancipating Word* (Minneapolis: Fortress Press, 2012). I have summarised the thoughts of Brueggemann in these points.

The second challenge is to engage in an urgent discussion on the meaning and future shape of civil society. Many of the institutions of our times that have helped sustain and provide guidance are increasingly being shunned or challenged, not least the church. Others include the professions, the parliaments, politicians, and the law. Although the recent controversy in the United Kingdom concerning phone hacking has brought to account certain practices of media owners, the media in general reports to no-one, claiming immunity as a free press essential to a democracy. Lindsay Tanner, in his book, *Sideshow: Dumbing Down Democracy*, claims that the media is interested in a sensational quick word or opinion, rather than reporting facts and engaging in bi-partisan dialogue and discussion.[26] Recent debates in the Federal parliament have been no more than personal attacks on the integrity of individuals, and since the September 2013 election distribution of details in key policy areas has been severely restricted. The growth in continuous television news coverage and the steady decline in print journalism are contributing to a further dumbing down of public discussion. While it is true that new forms of social media may help to address the challenge and improve discussion, there is little evidence to suggest that this is helping to modify the propaganda coming from major Australian newspapers.

In addressing the future of the secular state, Rowan Williams discusses the dilemmas of the secular state by suggesting that, like monochrome religious regimes, the secular state is struggling to maintain an identity. He says that those who call themselves secularists speak about freedom and equality, yet seek to deny a religious contribution to the debates, while their own ideology or prejudice is acceptable at any level.

The same issue is discussed by Brain Trainor in *Sacred Precedes Secular* when he calls on the State to shift from being a neutral overlord on the sacred/secular distinction to a position of active engagement, even ownership of a faith distinction that points beyond humanity. The State's role is to adjudicate impartially between the various cultural and religious structures and beliefs, to seek common threads and create a society that recognises difference in belief, but also a common commitment to a sustainable and coherent community.

---

26. Lindsay Tanner, *Sideshow: Dumbing Down Democracy* (Melbourne: Scribe Publications, 2011).

Williams, like Trainor, also argues that the public and private interconnection is 'enriched in the context of larger commitments and vision, and if forgotten or repressed by a supposedly neutral ideology of the public space, immense damage is done to the moral energy of a liberal society.'[27]

Each of the Gospel writers spoke into the context and the culture of their day. Language, imagery, parables and testimonies would have resonated with those to whom they spoke. This second challenge then for the Church today is to find a way to speak. A fresh way that speaks into the culture and with the culture of Australian society, where increasing numbers are two to three generations away from any meaningful contact with the Christian faith or the Church and any understanding of how the Christian heritage has shaped significantly who we are today. Walter Brueggemann says it with these words:

> Prophetic preaching is an effort to imagine the world as though YHWH, the creator of heaven and earth, the Father of our Lord Jesus Christ whom we Christians name as Father, Son and Spirit, is a real character and a defining agent in the world.[28]

How then do we speak about salvation, redemption, and divine love to a community that does not speak the language of belief and faith? How does one speak about the divine presence in Jesus without limiting Christian faith to the private sphere? Like the early gospel writers, the telling of the Christ event and the story of God's unending presence in the world cannot be separated or divorced from the institutions and principalities and powers that make up the secular context, a large number of which can be traced back to Christian principles and initiatives. It is important to note also that the secular world offers much that Christians accept, including many potential avenues and pathways for the good ordering of society. The church should applaud and acknowledge where advances in health, education and housing have contributed to improving the human condition, while not allowing itself to be seduced into embracing

---

27. Williams, *Faith in the Public Square*, 305.
28. Brueggemann, *Prophetic Imagination*, 23.

a non-critical approach when exploitation and abuse allow the powerful and wealthy to accumulate greater wealth at the expense of the poor. It needs to be remembered that eighty per cent of global wealth is controlled by twenty per cent of the world's population.

The third challenge for the churches and the agencies is to increase their own level of research in order to inform themselves, to differentiate between a Christian approach and the mainstream, and to engage in discussion that is about more than their own privilege or position. Building relationships with the universities and the think tanks, such as the Australia Institute, is one way of doing this and, in conjunction with the tools of economics and sociology, will enable cheap criticism to be debunked and raise the level of the church's contribution. A joint report in April 2009, titled 'Building financial health and wellbeing for disadvantaged Australians in the wake of the Global Financial Crisis', by Anglicare Australia, Catholic Social Services Australia, Uniting Care Australia, and the Salvation Army, provided the necessary data for the Federal government to accept the advice of the networks for urgent funds to protect the most vulnerable in the community. The report highlighted the additional costs that would be incurred if support were not forthcoming. Clearly, the Global Financial Crisis affected everyone, some more profoundly than others. Our standard of living, however, is sustained by the losses of others. In many places, infrastructure is lacking and moving forward restricted by the failure of those with resources to share them with others. This elephant in the room is still silent.

The fourth challenge is global urbanisation and the need to address growing income disparity and demands for energy. While Melbourne speaks about building an $8 billion tunnel, the rest of the state misses out on infrastructure and more young people leave rural homes and move to our increasingly large metropolitan cities. In many places in rural Australia, it is the church that stays, although under great duress. Think how much better education, health, housing, and transport could be if our approach to the future were less about urban growth and instead more about rural sustainability. What are the key principles of a more just and humane society other than wealth creation? Let our churches and agencies engage in this discussion with rigour and together, as the body of Christ called to serve the world. The Global Financial Crisis of 2008 identified major weaknesses in a free market approach without proper government intervention and engagement. While claims can be made that many have benefited from the free market, the Global Financial Crisis revealed the presence of enormous greed, inequality, and failure both of the system and of government oversight.

The fifth challenge is to recognise and acknowledge where the divine presence is at work outside the church and for the church to seek help from outside its own resources in order to strengthen its own mission and life. Christian faith may not provide all the answers to the social and ethical issues of the day, nor should we assume the secular or humanist option is necessarily better. As church and Christians, however, we are called to engage in all aspects of life that impinge on God's creation. Nourished by our own tradition, the opportunity is there for the church to be a robust and passionate advocate for a better world, while recognising the work of those who, although they do not share a Christian faith perspective, also seek the common good.

The Anglican Church's commitment to justice is not to be understood as merely alleviating poverty and challenging corrupt and dehumanising policies of today's empires. Justice should embrace God's vision, God's wisdom, and be grounded in the church's worship and prayer life.

Forum for Theology in the World Vol 1 No 2/2014

Social Concern in the Tradition of the Uniting Church in Australia

Mark Zirnsak

Social concern is at the heart of the Uniting Church in Australia's understanding of the Christian faith and the Gospel. This was made clear right from the start when the Uniting Church in Australia was formed in 1977 with the Statement to the Nation at the inaugural Assembly:

> People of the Congregational, Methodist and Presbyterian Churches have united. A new church has been born.
>
> We, who are members of the first Assembly of the Uniting Church in Australia address the people of Australia in this historic moment. The path to unity has been long and at times difficult, but we believe this unity is a sign of the reconciliation we seek for the whole human race.
>
> We acknowledge with gratitude that the churches from which we have come have contributed in various ways to the life and development of this nation. A Christian responsibility to society has always been regarded as fundamental to the mission of the Church. In the Uniting Church our response to the Christian gospel will continue to involve us in social and national affairs.
>
> We are conscious of our responsibilities within and beyond this country. We particularly acknowledge our responsibilities as one branch of the Christian church

within the region of South-East Asia and the Pacific. In these contexts we make certain affirmations at the time of our inauguration.

We affirm our eagerness to uphold basic Christian values and principles, such as the importance of every human being, the need for integrity in public life, the proclamation of truth and justice, the rights for each citizen to participate in decision-making in the community, religious liberty and personal dignity, and a concern for the welfare of the whole human race.

We pledge ourselves to seek the correction of injustices wherever they occur. We will work for the eradication of poverty and racism within our society and beyond. We affirm the rights of all people to equal educational opportunities, adequate health care, freedom of speech, employment or dignity in unemployment if work is not available. We will oppose all forms of discrimination which infringe basic rights and freedoms.

We will challenge values which emphasise acquisitiveness and greed in disregard of the needs of others and which encourage a higher standard of living for the privileged in the face of the daily widening gap between the rich and poor.

We are concerned with the basic human rights of future generations and will urge the wise use of energy, the protection of the environment and the replenishment of the earth's resources for their use and enjoyment.

Finally we affirm that the first allegiance of Christians is God, under whose judgment the policies and actions of all nations must pass. We realise that sometimes this allegiance may bring us into conflict with the rulers of our day. But our Uniting Church, as an institution within the nation, must constantly stress the universal values which must find expression in national policies if humanity is to survive. We pledge ourselves to hope and work for a nation whose goals are not guided by self-interest alone, but by concern for the welfare of all persons everywhere–the family of the One God–the God made known in Jesus of Nazareth the One who gave His life for others.

In the spirit of His self-giving love we seek to go forward.

This commitment to social concern within the public expression of the Uniting Church in Australia has been built on over time, as successive Assemblies have passed resolutions of a very wide range of issues, from justice for Indigenous Australians to global disarmament, from the treatment of asylum seekers to climate change.

Two of the more recent positions worthy of note as keynote positions for the Uniting Church:

- In 2006 the National Assembly meeting adopted *Dignity in Humanity—Recognising Christ in Every Person*. The statement was significant as it explicitly committed the Uniting Church in Australia to support a human rights framework through its understanding of the Christian faith. In this document the Uniting Church stated its belief that all people:

> ... are created in the image of God who is three persons in open, joyful interaction. The image of God that is reflected in human life, the form of life that corresponds to God, is the human community—all people—finding its life and sustenance in relationship.

> Thus, the Uniting Church believes that every person is precious and entitled to live with dignity because they are God's children, and that each person's life and rights need to be protected or the human community (and its reflection of God) and all people are diminished.

> We believe that Christians are called to love their neighbour as they love themselves and to extend that love

even to enemies. It is the love of God in Christ Jesus which motivates us to live out this calling by working for peace with justice in our church, our communities and the world. The recognition of human rights is an affirmation of the dignity of all people and essential for achieving peace with justice.

- *An Economy of Life* was adopted in 2009. It was a statement that committed the Uniting Church to ecological well-being and to reposition our economic system to place the well-being of people at the centre over the pursuit of profit. It lamented consumerism and materialism and saw them as antithetical to what is necessary for a healthy and sustainable world.

Living out its social concern

The Uniting Church in Australia gives life to its social concerns, not just through public expressions of its faith, but also through action.

The UnitingCare network, the community service arm of the Uniting Church in Australia, is one of the largest providers of community services in Australia. The network employs 35,000 staff providing services, supported by 24,000 volunteers, to more than two million people each year in 1300 sites in every State and Territory in remote, regional and urban Australia.

UnitingWorld provides a key part of the Uniting Church in Australia's engagement globally. Its Relief and Development Unit supports our overseas partners as they enable marginalised communities to live healthy and well-resourced lives. It focuses on building the capacity of our partners and their communities. It assists them in overcoming poverty and injustice, realising their fundamental human rights and developing long-term, sustainable livelihoods.

The Church Connections Unit of UnitingWorld stands alongside and supports partner churches in their life and witness and helps Australians see the world through our partners' eyes. This reciprocal engagement brings fresh understanding and renewed faith. The Unit develops, encourages and leads the Uniting Church's partnership in mission with churches overseas, especially in Asia, the Pacific and Africa.

The Uniting Church also maintains an employed social justice arm, with more staff than those employed directly in social justice roles by any other denomination. These staff members are directed to address the structural causes of injustice in our society and our world. They perform this function in a variety of ways, from resourcing church members to be active campaigners for social justice, engaging with governments and corporations and speaking on behalf of the church membership on social justice issues.

In the Victorian and Tasmanian Synod, we have nearly 5,000 people who connect directly with the social justice unit on a variety of issues and take action using the resources produced by the unit.

Key social issues for the churches today

In terms of the key issues I think we as churches face in Australia, my broad view is we need to tackle an increasingly inward-looking society that is being encouraged relentlessly to act selfishly and look after number one. There is a constant barrage about the financial struggle we all face and almost everyone is encouraged to see themselves as a 'battler', no matter how high their income in a global and historical perspective. That is not to say that there is not a disturbingly large group of people in real material hardship in Australia, but I struggle to accept a couple, without children, and with a combined income of over $200,000 are really on 'Struggle Street'.

The expression of this inward-looking concern for self finds expression in public policy through cuts to the humanitarian intake of refugees, cuts to the aid budget to fund road building projects in eastern State capitals, a planned massive increase in military spending, a desire to free-ride off the efforts of other countries in addressing climate change, and the desire of the wealthy to hang onto every benefit and hand-out from government they have had access to, no matter how unjustified it might be or even how poorly it makes sense even from the frame of economics. At its heart the Christian faith links our love of God to our love of our 'neighbours'. In our globalised world we should be encouraging Australian Christians to see their neighbours not just as the people in their local communities, not just in their State or Territory, not just other Australians, but all people across the globe.

The challenge of loving our neighbour in our world dominated by neo-liberal economic thinking is very difficult indeed. The system sets people up to compete against each other. The wellbeing of one group is often dependent on the suffering and misery of another. For example, consider the case of struggling fruit growers in Australia who are facing a possible wipe-out due to cheaper imports. One of the places those imports come from is Thailand, where there are low-paid jobs on farms producing the fruit and low-paid jobs in processing factories of the fruit. Many of these jobs are filled by millions of migrants from Burma. They desperately need these jobs, making them highly exploitable. Our global economic system pits the struggling Australian fruit grower and factory worker against the welfare of the financially impoverished Burmese migrant workers. It seems only one will be allowed to win. Thus, I find myself highly ambivalent to nationalistic 'Buy Australian' campaigns, to promote Australian jobs over jobs elsewhere. This kind of response unintentionally seems to encourage us to hate our global neighbours in order to look after those of the same nationality as us.

The role of the State

The role of the State in our community, in terms of regulating the behaviour of corporations and businesses and in providing services, is also an important area for engagement by churches. To my knowledge it is also an area where our theological reflection is not strongly developed. For those in the community who support the view of neo-liberal economics, the objective is to reduce the role of the State, turn public services into for-profit business opportunities and leave regulation of businesses to the market. While it is highly desirable to empower people to be self-sufficient and not dependent on welfare and to allow local communities to make decisions about their own future, this can become a cover for leaving people in great hardship unsupported and leaving communities without the services they need.

Churches ecumenically have supported the principle of 'subsidiarity', which means that things that can be done 'lower down' the level of social organisation should be done at that level. So if something is more appropriately done at the level of the individual, the family or the local community, it should be done there and not taken over by large organisations or by governments.[1] The purpose of this principle is to safeguard personal initiative and creativity. However, in the view of the Uniting Church in Australia this is balanced by the duty of governments to 'promote and protect human rights and "eliminate all violations of human rights and their causes, as well as obstacles to the enjoyment of these rights"'.[2] The Uniting Church in Australia has also formally recognised the role governments must play in regulating economic systems and structures to ensure 'human and ecological flourishing'[3] 'for the wellbeing of people and the planet'.

There is a lack of law enforcement on companies in Australia involved, directly or indirectly, in transnational criminal activities. Goods are freely imported into Australia where slavery, forced labour and human trafficking have been involved in their production. Until recently this included the online importation of child sexual abuse material by Australian Internet Service Providers. It is legal for Australian companies to pay small bribes to foreign officials for them to do their jobs, regardless of the wishes of the foreign government. Australia has been criticised over many years for its lack of effort in investigating the possibilities that Australian companies are involved in significant cases of paying large bribes overseas, with recent media investigations finally spurring Australian authorities to greater action. Funds stolen from the Papua New Guinea Government have been freely transferred into Australian banks and used to purchase properties in Queensland.[4] There are question marks about the extent to which Australian-based multinational corporations follow the practices of many other multinational corporations in tax evasion and tax avoidance activities through the use of subsidiaries in secrecy jurisdictions. Those worst impacted by this activity are developing countries, who, from estimates in Christian Aid research collectively

---

1. The Australian Episcopal Conference of the Roman Catholic Church, *A New Beginning: Eradicating Poverty in our World*, (Melbourne: HarperCollins, 1996), 10.
2. Uniting Church in Australia, *Dignity in Humanity: Recognising Christ in Every Person* (Sydney: The Uniting Church in Australia, 2006), 5.
3. Uniting Church in Australia, *An Economy of Life* (Sydney: the Uniting Church in Australia, 2009), 17-18.
4. Sam Koim, AUSTRAC Major Reporters Meeting, Sydney, 4 October 2012.

lose US$160 billion annually on just two types of common multinational corporate tax dodging.[5] That is more than developing countries collectively get in aid.

The importance of taxation in a just society

Australia collects too little tax to achieve the vision of a just and caring society. It collects too little by comparison with other OECD countries. It also collects too little to provide the services the Australian community should be able to expect for our national wealth and to effectively regulate the corporate sector.

In 2010 the OECD average tax collection as a proportion of Gross Domestic Product (GDP) was 33.8 per cent[6], with the Nordic countries, Austria, Belgium and France all collecting over 40 per cent of GDP in tax revenue. Further, other OECD countries are seeing their tax revenue as a proportion of GDP increase, with the average across OECD countries increasing from 34.1 percent of GDP in 2011 to 34.6 per cent in 2012. By comparison, total taxation revenue as a proportion of GDP in Australia was 26 per cent in the 2011/12 financial year. As a percentage of GDP, taxation revenue for the Commonwealth Government was 22 per cent, State Governments 4 per cent and Local Governments 1 per cent.[7] Australia's tax take is closer to that of Korea (27 per cent of GDP), the USA (24 per cent of GDP) and Chile (21 per cent of GDP). Australia's tax take as a proportion of GDP is at the lowest it has been for 20 years.

Analysis by conservative economic bodies like the International Monetary Fund (IMF) show the Federal Government has choices and the spending cuts are a choice not a necessity. The IMF Working Paper *Understanding Countries' Tax Efforts* released in November 2013 found that Australia was collecting only between 70-4 per cent of its

---

5. Andrew Hogg et al., *Death and Taxes: the True Toll of Tax Dodging* (London: Christian Aid, 2008), 2.
6. OECD Stats. Extract, 'Revenue Statistics—Comparative Table', http://stats.oecd.org/index.aspx.
7. Australian Bureau of Statistics, '5506.0 - Taxation Revenue, Australia, 2011-12', 30 April 2013, http://www.abs.gov.au/ausstats/abs@.nsf/Latestproducts/5506.0Main%20Features52011-12?opendocument&tabname=Summary&prodno=5506.0&issue=2011-12&num=&view=.

tax capacity. This was low compared to other wealthy countries such as France (96-8 per cent), Germany (79-84 per cent), Netherlands (80-7 per cent), New Zealand (78-80 per cent), Norway (87-92 per cent) and the UK (82-6 per cent). So if Australia were to increase its tax take by 10 per cent of its capacity to tax, to around the level of New Zealand and the UK, it would add $34 billion a year to government revenue. That would be almost enough to balance the current budget.

In the last 50 years Australia has been a low-tax country compared to most of the OECD countries. In the period 1965 to 2012, Australian government tax revenue peaked at 30 per cent of GDP for the period 2002-7.[8]

Tax reductions have favoured the wealthy

Further, much of the reduction in taxes in the last two decades has been for the benefit of the wealthiest Australians, increasing financial inequality in Australia. Research by The Australia Institute found the Federal Government would have had an additional $38 billion for last year's federal government budget and would have collected an extra $169 billion over the last seven years had it not been for unsustainable income tax cuts that were made in the lead-up to the Global Financial Crisis.[9] Australia's highest income earners got one of the largest tax cuts in the developed world in the past decade–surpassing the unfunded tax cuts of the US Bush Administration. In 2000 upper-middle income earners were taxed at an effective tax rate of 38.3 per cent, which dropped to 31.7 per cent in 2010.[10] Of the $169 billion in tax cuts given out in the last seven years, $71 billion went to the highest 10 per cent of income earners. The top 10 per cent of income earners got more than the bottom 80 per cent.[11]

In Australia, over a period of 30 years the corporate tax rate has been slashed from 46 per cent to 30 per cent.

---

8. OECD Stats. Extract, 'Revenue Statistics—Comparative Table', http://stats.oecd.org/index.aspx
9. Matt Grudnoff, *Tax Cuts that Broke the Budget*, (Canberra: The Australia Institute, Policy Brief Number 51, May 2013), 1.
10. George Megalogenis, 'How our rich were given some of the world's biggest tax cuts', *The Australian*, 21 September 2011.
11. Grudnoff, *Tax Cuts*, 1.

The cut in corporate tax rates also puts pressure on the top marginal personal income tax rate, otherwise rich individuals will find ways to reclassify their ordinary income as corporate income. Thus in Australia, the top marginal tax rate has declined from 75 per cent in 1951 to 45 per cent now. By comparison, the average tax rate (total tax as a proportion of income) for a worker earning the male average wage in Australia was steady at around 22 per cent from the 1970s to the 2000s. The marginal tax rate (the rate of tax paid on an additional dollar of income) for the same worker averaged around 35 per cent in that period.[12] So it is the wealthiest that have benefited from tax rate reductions.

The churches need to be engaged in the economic sphere

Given the key cross-cutting issues of the increasing selfishness and the importance of the role of the State in service provision and regulation, churches concerned about social issues should be engaged in the economic sphere. It is a positive sign that representatives of churches are increasing their participation in the economic debates and consultations with government, but often are excluded in being reported by mainstream media. I am guessing a lot of journalists would currently question what qualifications churches have to comment on economic issues.

As examples of churches' participation in economic consultations, a church representative was the only non-business representative in recent consultations by the previous Federal Government on reforms to Australia's transfer pricing laws for multinational corporations. Churches were represented on the Assistant Treasurer's expert group on consultations regarding addressing multinational corporate tax dodging. The ecumenical campaign Micah Challenge also made a submission to the consultation process on this issue.

Churches are represented on Treasury consultations with business and the community on a range of tax related issues.

However, there remains a significant challenge for churches to assist their members in making the connections between the Christian faith and economic issues. A further challenge is to ensure

---

12. Richard Warburton and Peter Hendy, 'International Comparison of Australian Taxes', The Treasury, 2006.

that making such connections is not, and is not seen to be, the churches being politically partisan, but acting very much from an understanding of the Gospel.

The challenge of the church being heard in society

I think there is a real danger in assessing the churches' engagement in social issues based on pick-up in the mainstream media. Privately owned mainstream media are hardly organisations run with the purpose of providing objective news. They do actively push their own agendas and exclude those agendas they do not support. For example, the largest media corporation in Australia, News Corp, according to a study by the US Government Accountability Office, has more subsidiaries in secrecy jurisdictions than any other company in the ASX 100 by a long way. In 2008 it had 146 subsidiaries, including 62 in the British Virgin Islands, 33 in the Cayman Islands and two in Switzerland.[13] Further, News Corporation was accused of tax dodging in the late 1980s in the recent book *Treasure Islands: Tax Havens and the Men who Stole the World*.[14] So when we released a report into the ASX 100 companies with subsidiaries in secrecy jurisdictions in May 2013, it made front page of the Fairfax newspapers, but did not rate a mention in News Corp newspapers.

A multinational media corporation engaged in tax dodging and whose owner benefits greatly from the status quo is extremely unlikely to give much space to those church-affiliated people who wish to speak out on issues of social justice and who wish to see significant reform to economic systems for the benefit of the majority at the cost of the super-rich.

Further, it is clear that at times some media outlets run specific campaigns targeting the churches on various issues and that some journalists are less than sympathetic towards the views of churches.

Many churches challenge one of the central tenets of neo-liberal economic thinking, that material consumption can be equated to

---

13. US Government Accountability Office, *International Taxation. Large US Corporations and Federal Contractors with Subsidiaries in Jurisdictions Listed as Tax Havens or Financial Privacy Jurisdictions*, December 2008.
14. Nicholas Shaxson, *Treasure Islands. Tax Havens and the Men who Stole the World*, (London: The Bodley Head, 2011), 10.

human happiness. Given that private media are financially dependent on advertising revenue, the churches' critique of consumerism is a direct attack on this funding base.

This does not mean giving up on mainstream media, but recognising their limitations and making greater use of other forms of media and communication with church members and the wider community.

The struggle between being distinctive and relevant

In the area of social issues, many churches wish to be both distinctive and relevant at the same time. However, these two aims can work against each other. There is a danger of being irrelevant where churches decide to go it alone on a social issue, rather than being willing to be part of a broader movement. Churches need to remain true to who they are and the core of their faith tradition, but this often is not a barrier to being able to work within broader movements, even if the other organisations in the movement share the same social goal from different motivations. At the same time, it is important churches remain true to who they are in the tactics they use. Love of our opponents may at times mean we do not work with organisations who adopt an approach of hatred towards those opposed to the social outcomes they are seeking.

Seeking to be distinctive can be a barrier to even being able to work ecumenically.

Churches can no longer rely on having a special place in society to be able to claim relevance. Churches must demonstrate their credibility by undertaking thorough research and not just make moral pronouncements on issues without the backing of such research if they wish to be taken seriously in public debates.

I believe Fr Brennan raises two areas where many Christians recently did themselves a disservice in the positions they took, undermining the churches' relevance on social issues in the Australian community. The two issues have been around the legal defence to carry out religiously motivated discrimination and the defence of people being able to incite religiously motivated hatred.

Churches and the defence of racial discrimination
On the former there is a very legitimate discussion to be had about how a balance needs to be struck between defending people from harmful discrimination while offering maximum protection to the right of freedom of religion. In 2008 the then Labor Victorian Government undertook a review of the exemptions and exceptions under the *Equal Opportunity Act 1995*. Section 77 provided an exception to both individuals and organisations to be able to carry out discrimination that would otherwise be unlawful provided the discrimination is in keeping with the person's genuinely held religious beliefs. This included racial discrimination, discrimination against people with disabilities, against union members, against carers and against women who were breastfeeding. The initial position adopted by many churches, including the Catholic Church and the Uniting Church Synod of Victoria and Tasmania, was to demand this right to carry out any form of discrimination consistent with a person's or organisation's religious beliefs should be maintained. It was simply impossible to offer any justification why churches believed that harmful racial discrimination should be legally protected provided the discrimination was religiously motivated. Given the important role churches had played in the civil rights movement in the US on racial discrimination against Afro-Americans and against apartheid in South Africa and the well-developed theological condemnation of racial discrimination, it was highly damaging to the churches' public standing to then be demanding legal protection for religiously-motivated racial discrimination. It was an even more puzzling position to be defending when none of churches doing so carried out religiously motivated discrimination against people on the basis of their race, because they had a disability, they were a union member or a carer or they were breastfeeding. It created a perception that the churches were willing to defend any legal privilege the State was willing to grant them regardless of whether they actually needed it and regardless of possible harm to others in the community.

There are good reasons to seek to limit the forms of harmful discrimination in our community. The World Health Organisation had formed the view based on available research that 'many health disparities are rooted in fundamental social structural inequalities, which are inextricably related to racism and other forms of discrimination in society.'[15] A 2007 study by VicHealth into discrimination against migrant and refugee communities found that there is a strong relationship between exposure to discrimination and poor mental health, especially depression. The finding was further supported by a review of 138 empirical quantitative population-based studies of self-reported racism and health. The studies showed an association between self-reported racism and ill health for oppressed racial groups after adjustment for a range of confounders. The strongest and most consistent findings are for negative mental health outcomes.[16] The evidence from longitudinal studies also suggests that being subjected to racism precedes ill health rather than visa versa.[17]

In the end the churches in Victoria changed their position. The Catholic Church only sought exception from the anti-discrimination laws for acts of religiously motivated discrimination on the basis of religious belief or activity, sex, sexual orientation, lawful sexual activity, marital status, parental status and gender identity. The Victorian Government agreed to this position. The Uniting Church, Synod of Victoria and Tasmania, indicated it was supportive of the State limiting the harmful forms of religiously-motivated discrimination much further in a resolution passed by its Synod meeting in 2010.

The Christian community and incitement to religious hatred
In the case of the Victorian *Racial and Religious Tolerance Act*, I will disagree with Fr Brennan that the law 'hindered rather than helped religious and social harmony'. Our monitoring of extremist groups that seek to incite racial and religious hatred suggest such groups are far more numerous and active in NSW and Queensland where the legal restrictions on incitement to racial and religious hatred are more limited. Our monitoring also suggested these groups found that the *Racial and Religious Tolerance Act* curbed their ability to promote their message in Victoria and seek new recruits.

The case of Catch the Fire Ministries was again an example of many Christians behaving poorly, leaping to the defence of a

---

15. VicHealth, *More than Tolerance: Embracing Diversity for Health* (Melbourne: Victorian Health Promotion Foundation, 2007).
16. Yin Paradies, 'A Systematic Review of Empirical Research on Self-reported Racism and Health', *International Journal of Epidemiology* 35 (2006), 888.
17. Yin Paradies, 'A Systematic Review of Empirical Research on Self-reported Racism and Health', *International Journal of Epidemiology* 35 (2006), 895.

Christian group against the Muslim community with little knowledge or understanding of the facts of the case. Pastor Danny Nalliah had come to our attention in late 2001 when one of our congregations expressed concern about brochures they were being asked to distribute which carried an endorsement from Pastor Nalliah. The brochures called on church members to get a map of their local area and circle 'Satan's strongholds' which included mosques and temples of Freemasons, Buddhists and Hindus and to take the map 'to your church and ask your intercessors, through the pastor, to pull these strongholds down.' It needs to be remembered that the context of this activity, and the subsequent activity that was the subject of civil action by the Islamic Council of Victoria, was that it was being carried out just after the September 11 terrorist attack in the US. The Muslim community in Australia found itself on the receiving end of a substantial increase in acts of violence, discrimination, harassment, and verbal abuse in public by strangers. Muslim women were spat at, had their hijabs pulled off, had dogs set on them, had rocks thrown at them, had people try and run them off the road and threaten them with rape.[18]

On 17 December 2004 the Victorian Civil and Administrative Tribunal (VCAT) found that Catch the Fire Ministries had sought to incite 'hatred against, serious contempt for, revulsion of or severe ridicule of' Muslims through the seminar it held, and had sought to 'incite a feeling of hatred towards Muslims' through an article published in its newsletter, and an article it had published on its website incited 'hatred against and serious contempt for people who are Muslims.' At the seminar organised by Catch the Fire Ministries on 9 March 2002, Pastor Daniel Scot said things about Muslims that were disturbingly similar in form to anti-Semitic speeches and literature from Europe in the late 1800s and early 1900s.[19] Pastor Scot's presentation at the seminar and anti-Semitic speeches and literature from the late 1800s and early 1900s share the following false claims about the people of the faith being targeted because:

---

18. Human Rights and Equal Opportunity Commission, *Ismae—Listen: National Consultations on Eliminating Prejudice Against Arab and Muslim Australians* (Sydney: Human Rights and Equal Opportunity Commission, 2004), 43-64.
19. George Bernstein, *Anti-Semitism in Imperial Germany, 1871-1913: Selected Documents* (Michigan: Teachers College, Columbia University, 1973), 249- 258, 282, 296, 310, 316, 337, 352-353; Allan Gould, *What did they Think of the Jews* (New Jersey: J. Aronson, 1991), 223.

- Their faith teaches them that it is good for them to kill people not of their faith;
- Their faith teaches that those who kill people of other faiths are ranked above others;
- Their faith teaches them not to be friends with anyone outside of their faith;
- They seek to deceive non-believers about the true nature of their faith;
- They use their money to fulfil their desire for power;
- People in the media are afraid of them and so do not report accurately on what they do;
- They have control over parts of government; and
- They seek world domination.

There is similarity in that both the anti-Semitism and the anti-Muslim preaching of Pastor Scot rely on stereotyping, scare-mongering, scapegoating and making claims about the other faith's religious texts. However, it should be recognised that anti-Semitism has a unique nature and I am not suggesting an equivalence between the history of anti-Semitism and the anti-Muslim preaching of Pastor Scot. At the same time, despite the similarity between Pastor Scot's anti-Muslim preaching at the seminar and claims made in historical anti-Semitic material, many Christians and even churches lined up to throw their support behind Catch the Fire Ministries.

Fortunately support for Catch the Fire Ministries started to wane after Pastor Danny Nalliah caused a series of public outrages. In 2007 it was revealed that Pastor Nalliah had given a speech to the anti-Semitic organisation, the League of Rights.[20] Then Pastor Nalliah caused public outrage by suggesting the February 2009 Victorian bushfires were due to God removing His protection from Victoria in response to the Victorian Parliament decriminalising abortion.[21] The bushfires had claimed 173 lives. Even long standing supporter of Pastor Nalliah, Peter Costello publicly distanced himself from Pastor Nalliah over the comments. Pastor Nalliah again made himself the centre of controversy by suggesting the Queensland floods in January 2011 were God 'trying to get our attention'[22] because Foreign Minister Kevin Rudd had called on Israel to join the Nuclear Non-Proliferation Treaty and open its nuclear facilities to UN inspectors.

To Pastor Nalliah's credit, it would appear that after the settlement of the case with the Islamic Council of Victoria he has not sought to promote the same material against the Muslim community that gave rise to the civil action before VCAT and later the Supreme Court.

The way forward

The Uniting Church in Australia has seen from its beginning that the Gospel calls Christians to be engaged in social concerns, both theologically and through practical action. The Uniting Church in Australia has recognised that for its concerns about social issues to be taken seriously, it needs to conduct credible research to back up its theological principles. More broadly, for churches to be a relevant voice on social issues they need to work ecumenically, which will become increasingly important if church attendance across many churches continues to decline. On major social issues there will also be a growing need to work with secular organisations that seek similar outcomes on the same issues. The churches in Australia have their work cut out for them if they wish to influence Australian society to have a greater 'love of neighbour' both at home and abroad.

Forum for Theology in the World Vol 1 No 2/2014

Social Justice in the Coptic Orthodox Church

Shenouda Boutros

The Coptic Orthodox Church belongs to the Oriental Orthodox family, which also includes the Syrians, Armenians, Ethiopians, Eritrean and Indian. The Coptic Orthodox Church is a Trinitarian, Scriptural, Sacramental Apostolic Church. The term Coptic means Egyptian and is a derivative of the Greek word "Agaeptos". The Coptic Church in Egypt has a very ancient beginning. Christ himself visited Egypt during his infancy and spent about three-and-a-half years in Egypt. The flight of the Holy Family to Egypt is found in the writings of Hippolytus of Rome. He was a theologian, active church leader and a biblical commentator during the early 3rd century. He indicates that the Holy Family stayed in Egypt for three years and six months. He may have received early local traditions within the Christian church in Egypt just over 200 years after the death of Christ.

Christianity in Egypt traces its Apostolic introduction to St Mark the Evangelist who came to Alexandria between 42-44AD, though some sources say around 60AD. According to Eusebius, who wrote his Ecclesiastical History in the first quarter of the fourth century, tradition records that Mark came to Egypt in the first or third year of the reign of the Roman Emperor Claudius. The Church of Alexandria (Coptic Church) in the first century established the great Catechetical School of Alexandria around 180AD, and for the next two centuries played a pre-eminent role in many of the theological controversies and defining the orthodox faith. The Coptic Church produced giants in theology and leadership of the universal church, such as St Demetrius, St Alexanderos, St Athanasius, Clement of Alexandria and St Cyril.

However the role of the Church of Alexandria on the world stage began to change dramatically after the Council of Chalcedon in 425 AD, after which time the Coptic Church became increasingly isolated and persecuted by the Byzantine Empire and the Chalcedonian churches. In fact the Church in Egypt from the beginning until the time of Constantine's Edict of Milan in 314 AD was heavily persecuted. Eusebius in his ecclesiastical history wrote about the martyrs of Egypt: 'These were most numerous at Alexandria, to which, as to a huge arena, God's noble champions were conducted from the whole of Egypt and the Thebaid.'[1] The only brief time in which Christianity in Egypt had any type of freedom from persecution and repression was for the period between 331 AD and 451 AD, about 100 years. But even that had periods of hardships and persecution in which the church hierarchy were often challenged and exiled.

The Arab conquest began in 639 AD under Amr ibn al-As. This came with some very heavy burdens for the Copts, such as very high taxes (*Jizya*, protection money). The Copts became *Dhimmi* (second class people, many converted to Islam, constant threats of imprisonment of clergy and hierarchy, confiscation of ecclesiastical treasures and churches, and erratic periodic periods of severe persecutions and martyrdom. When The Arab conquest began around 639 AD, 80 per cent of the population was Coptic (Christian). By the 12th century the Copts were 15 per cent of the population. The Muslim leaders had tried to eradicate all traces of the Coptic culture. The Coptic language itself was outlawed in the 8th century by Caliph Abd al-Malik ibn Marwan, who decreed that Arabic replace *Koine* Greek and Coptic as the sole administrative language. If people were found speaking Coptic, their tongues would be cut out. By the 17th century Coptic was no longer spoken and was something used only in the church liturgy.

Throughout the history of Egypt, the Copts have considered themselves the natives of Egypt and the descendants of the pharaohs. They have never been in a position of political control of their own country, but have always been under the yoke of an outside and imposed ruler. In modern times, the Copts continue to be severely persecuted, marginalised, with effectively no legal rights or political power. Early in 2013, during the revolution against Morsi, close to

---

1. Eusebius, *The History of the Church* (London: Penguin Books, 1989), 179.

one hundred churches and associated buildings were burned and destroyed. This is the setting in which the Coptic Church in Egypt finds itself.

Religion and faith play a very important part in the life of every Egyptian, both Muslim and Christian. The Coptic Church plays a central part in the life of the Copts. Today most Copts attend the liturgy and partake of communion regularly. Due to the fact that in their own country the Copts have been marginalised and persecuted and made to be second-class citizens, the result is that the Church for centuries has become their community and their social network. This in part comes from a sense of self-preservation. This is not to mean that the Copts isolate themselves from their community, but they are in some respects isolated and marginalised.

In Egypt there are very few social services offered by the government, and so there is a huge hole to fill both for the Christian and Muslim populations. As a result the Coptic Church has a very strong social service ministry in Egypt towards all, both Christian and Muslim. The Church supports the poor, giving millions in financial aid. The Church has orphanages, hospitals and rehabilitation centres, and supports widows and their children financially and by offering protection and education to their children. The Church offers development programs such as trade training, support to start a business, and many other services.

Education is an important priority for Copts, and the church has many schools, tutorial services and financial support for education. The Church also places much emphasis on Christian education through theological seminaries, Sunday school, and youth education. In Australia the Copts established schools very early on after settling here. Recently a theological college was established, St Athanasius Coptic Orthodox College. The Sunday School and Youth service is the center and focus of Church services.

The Coptic clergy play a very important part in the life of the Coptic Church; they have a hands-on pastoral approach. The priest is a part of every family and he is considered the father figure in every family.

Throughout its history the Coptic Church has occupied a very unique position in that it both officially and unofficially is the only body that speaks for and advocates for the Coptic minority.

However this can have its difficulties. Let me give a contemporary example. In the early 1970s under Anwar Sadat there was a move to Islamise Egypt and as a result many churches were attacked. The focal points of some attacks were buildings that Christians used for prayer and that had not received the necessary government approval. (In order for a church to be built it must receive presidential approval, a difficult thing to obtain).

On 6th November 1972, an attack took place in El Khanka on such a building. This of course angered the Copts and the Church was once again in a position where it had to advocate for itself and its people. The recently enthroned Pope Shenouda III of blessed memory (1971-2012) ordered some bishops and priests to march to the place and hold Mass. Such a march was viewed as a provocation by Muslims, and the building was attacked again.

The parliamentary committee tasked with investigating the attack noted that out of 1,442 church buildings in Egypt only 500 had the necessary governmental approval. It also noted that in the ten-year period from 1962 to 1972, 127 permits were given for church buildings and that only 68 of these were for the Coptic Church. These 68 included only 22 new and 46 renovation permits. The committee recommended a government solution to the problem, but none was undertaken.

The state and the Islamists competed on suggesting more laws that would guarantee the Islamisation of the country. Al Azhar proposed a law in 1977 for the implementation of shari'a in the country. The law included the implementation of the Islamic penal code and the death penalty for apostates. On 21 March 1977, a court ruled that shari'a was to be applied to Copts in their personal status cases, allowing men to marry four women and obtain divorce. The personal status law governing Copts was already a problem since Nasser's abolishment of the religious courts in 1955. Under law 462 of 1955, the application of non-Muslim personal status laws was limited only to those cases where the two parties belonged to the same religion. Furthermore, this involved only marriages and divorce. In all other issues, such as guardianship, inheritance, adoption and legal capacity, Islamic shari'a was applied to all Egyptians. There were many conspiracy theories at the time leveled against the Copts. In the absence of sufficient political representation responsibility for voicing Christian concerns on political and social issues fell primarily on the church and the Patriarch HH Pope Shenouda III.

The Patriarch irritated President Sadat when he protested against the government-sponsored Islamisation bill of 1977, which, if passed, would have made conversion from Islam to Christianity punishable by death, and the 1980 constitutional amendment making Islamic law the principal source of legislation. Sadat also regarded Pope Shenouda as a political opponent because he believed the Patriarch to be responsible for the embarrassing demonstrations against his government's Islamisation policies that he encountered on travels in the West. To silence the Patriarch and improve his own Islamic credentials in the face of mounting Islamic opposition to his regime Sadat chose to take drastic action against the Coptic Pope.

President Sadat publicly accused Pope Shenouda of being party to a CIA, German Christian Democratic Party and World Council of Churches conspiracy to establish a Christian state in Upper Egypt with its capital at Assiout and charged him with aiding Lebanon's besieged Christian community. Sadat decreed the dismissal of Shenouda as Patriarch and had him placed under house arrest at the remote Monastery of St Bishoy. One hundred and sixty Christians, including eight bishops and 16 priests, were arrested at the same time on the basis of Presidential Decree 143 of 1981 for allegedly threatening national unity and security. In April 1983 an Egyptian Court upheld the legality of the presidential decree deposing Pope Shenouda. Pope Shenouda remained under house arrest until 1985 when President Mubarak yielded to international pressure applied by human rights organisations such as Christian Solidarity International and Amnesty International. The detention of Pope Shenouda and the imprisonment of 160 Christians in 1981 effectively intimidated Church leaders from defending energetically the interests of the Christian community in the political arena.

The history of the Coptic Church is full of such stories in which the church hierarchy had to continually advocate for the social justice of their people, often with great cost.

In the diaspora

The Copts have integrated very well into their communities. For instance the Coptic churches are found spread out in different areas of Melbourne, unlike many other ethnic communities, the Copts have not settled in one particular area. They are most happy to be part of the wider community

The Coptic Church places great importance on its relationship with other churches. It is very ecumenically minded and is engaged at all levels of ecumenical discussion. HH Pope Tawadros II said recently in a meeting he had with Pope Francis, 'For us unity as Christians is the norm, and separation is the exception to that norm.'

Here in Australia the social services that the Coptic Church is involved in are many and varied, and considering how young the church is in Australia and its size, it reflects how important social service is to the Coptic Orthodox Church.

The following is a list of some of services:

Social work in Australia:
- Coptic Hope Charity (This is a charity fund that offers support to people on a regular ongoing basis, both in Egypt and Fiji, Australia and New Zealand, but also support for disasters and crises, eg Black Saturday, the recent destruction of churches and Coptic homes/businesses in Egypt etc.)
- Manna for life (feeding for the homeless)
- Support services for refugees and new migrants (we have a constant stream of new migrants and refugees, especially after the so-called Arab Spring. This includes finding housing, financial support, employment, picking them up from the airport, helping them find schools, etc.
- Crisis accommodation
- Financial assistance
- Schools
- Hostel for the elderly
- Serving the elderly and widows
- Prison ministry
- Hospital chaplaincy
- University chaplaincy
- Exodus (a youth outreach mission for those who are battling drugs etc.)
- Orphanage (in Fiji).

The Coptic Church is also involved in issues regarding the wider community, at all levels of the debate. For example in the abortion law reform debates of 2008 (Victoria), the Coptic Church made its position clear and was involved publically in the debate at all levels. Also concerning the issue of same sex marriage, the Church is involved in the debate at all levels. The Coptic Church in Australia is lobbying hard for the justice of the Copts in Egypt, for their protection and rights. The Coptic Church places great importance on social services and offers much more than just spiritual service.

Response to Fr Frank Brennan

Fr Frank said:

> Our challenge always is to assist society's decision makers to form their conscience, inform their consciences and to those consciences be true, including the discharge of all appropriate obligations of political life including attention to the electorate's wishes, party policy, and the national interest.

I wholeheartedly agree with this statement, and I believe this is the challenge of the church in Australia, a most important role.

Fr Frank went on to say: 'As Christians, we can bring God's blessings to all in our world, even those who have no time for our Churches and not much interest in our Lord.'

A most beautiful and profound statement and I firmly believe that the church in Australia has this most important duty and role to play. But in order for us as Christians to have an effect to bring God's blessing into our world, I believe we must be united in our efforts and in our moral/ethical positions.

And this of course is probably our biggest challenge. As the Lord said, 'If a kingdom is divided against itself, that kingdom cannot stand. And if a house is divided against itself, that house will not be able to stand' (Mark 3:24-25).

Clearly dogmatically we have differences but perhaps what is even a more significant problem from a social justice perspective is the problem that as churches we cannot agree upon moral and ethical issues. So the problem arises that if we as Christians cannot agree upon moral issues how then can we as Fr Frank rightly said, 'assist society's decision makers to form their conscience, inform their consciences and to those consciences be true,' and therefore 'Bring God's blessing into our world'?

An example is the highly contentious issue, the debate on same-sex marriages. I understand that the reality of all Christian churches having the one mind on this issue is becoming most difficult if not impossible, although I firmly believe that we can 'do all things through Christ who strengthens me'. Here is an issue on which Christians have many different views, as there are different denominations. So the challenge as Christians and the Churches collectively is how can we come to an agreement in order to have a united front and 'bring God's blessing into our world.' I don't have any easy answers but to me this seems to be our biggest challenge. Fifty-sixty years ago I think it would be safe to assume that all churches would have had the same view and teachings with regards to pre-marital sex. Now I'm not so sure.

I know that what I am about to say will not be popular, nor will it be accepted by the majority, but my conscience and convictions inspire me to say such things. We need to go back with sincerity and honesty to the teachings of God and allow His Holy Spirit to guide us. With regard to the issue of homosexuality and same-sex unions, it is clear that modern day scholarship, and here I am referring to academic theological studies, has lead many to a different understanding of homosexual relations, different at least to the traditional churches such as the Orthodox and Catholic churches. This is in part due to modern scholarship, which has become highly critical of the Holy Scriptures and so evades the scriptures and in its place puts hypothesis and conjecture to support alternative views. Compassion and care and justice should be given to all. However the churches' role must be to stand up for what is morally right and clearly say what is wrong. Fr Frank said:

> I called a lesbian Catholic I knew who had children with her partner and she told me that she was a lesbian and always would be; that she was Catholic and always

would be; that the clergy should get over this idea that they were gatekeepers to the gospels and the sacraments because the key message was that God is love.

I agree with this person to an extent in that it is not only the clergy who are gatekeepers to the gospels and the sacraments, but it should be the whole church, everyone who considers himself/herself a Christian, it is their duty to live the Gospel and to ensure that they are the 'light to the world', especially if this is going against the tide.

Fr Frank said, 'Religion is much less relevant now to the civil definition of marriage'. This may well be true, but this is no reason for the church and her people to change their position on an understanding of marriage clearly taught by Christ.

As I said before I have no easy answers and I know that the majority will not agree with what I have said, however the point I would like to make is that the greatest challenge we have as churches in Australia is to be united in our outlook towards current social and cultural issues. If we can be united then I think we can achieve great things and as Fr Frank said, 'As Christians, we can bring God's blessings to all in our world, even those who have no time for our churches and not much interest in our Lord.'

The Importance of Knowing Our Christian Social Traditions

Margaret Coffey

Christian social teaching for me falls into two categories. The one is the relatively new and evolving body of 'canonical' Catholic social teaching which I encountered first as part of my education and background. The other is the broad culture of Christian perspectives on the sacredness that inheres in every human being, in social relations and in creation. As I have discovered, perspectives on the social meaning of Christian belief are richly expressed in the foundation stories and the histories of social engagement of diverse denominations and movements. And so are the difficulties attached to renewing and re-energising Christian communities in their social roles.

Over the last 120 years or so, that canonical teaching has emerged in a series of papal writings in response to contemporary conditions. Elements of this body of responses to the economic and political dimensions of individual and social relationships have been elaborated into principles, essentially out of the vision of the human person presented in the Scriptures, a vision that always situates the person in a human community. It's invariably astonishing to be reminded just how strongly such themes have been at work in the very roots of the Christian story–and of the long history of reflection on them in both Jewish and Christian traditions. But the origins of what we understand now as that body of Catholic social teaching are quite near to us, and its working out through the decades of the twentieth century actually engages quite intimately with the lives of many Australian Catholics. On reflection I realise that Catholic social teaching entered my consciousness in turn by osmosis and in dollops of learning from experience, and I note that there have been stages in my understanding of this evolving heritage. I think it is fair to say that many of us, Catholics and otherwise, are on a new threshold of understanding–due in part to Pope Francis and in part simply to the changing character of the challenges our world presents us.

The historical circumstances that drove towards the definition of principles we recognise today as lynchpins of a more systematic Catholic social teaching arose in particular in the nineteenth century. Then, the important factors were industrialisation, in the context of the continuing rise of nation states, and also of ideology as an organising principle behind politics and various competing visions of society. (In the nineteenth century the ideology that really disturbed the papal viewpoint was socialism, but so did capitalism, certainly by the end of the century.)

In 1836 Frederic Ozanam, a French layman and the founder of the St Vincent de Paul Society, observed:

> What divides mankind nowadays, is no longer a political problem; it is a social issue. It is knowing which will prevail, the spirit of selfishness or the spirit of sacrifice, whether the society will be merely a great exploitation for the benefit of the strongest or the dedication of each individual to the good of all and especially to the protection of the weak.

Catholic social teaching as we know it today emerged in some important sense in recognition of the social issue as described by Frederic Ozanam.

Pope Leo XIII's 1891 encyclical *Rerum Novarum (The Worker Question)*, which is commonly held to be the initiating document of contemporary Catholic social teaching, taught principles about the relationship between labour and capital. It expressed many ideas which Ozanam had held and some of which had already animated for decades the growth of a Catholic lay movement committed to ensuring that justice accompanied charity. The St Vincent de Paul Society, founded in Paris in 1833, was very quickly inserted in parishes world-wide. The first St Vincent de Paul Society meeting in Australia took place in Melbourne on 5 March 1854, just twenty-one years after Ozanam brought together the foundation group. It is interesting to reflect that during the latter half of the 19th century there was a strand at work in Catholic colonial lives with the capacity of tying together social justice, charity and their actual social experience (though it is true to say there was a tension in the Society's tradition).

One of the fascinating aspects of Catholic social teaching as it emerged through the nineteenth century is precisely the vigour it gained from its engagement with the social conditions and intellectual currents of the time. People like Frederic Ozanam did not take refuge in nostalgia or atavism. They were animated by how the Gospel spoke to their times, and by the intellectual debates about them. (Ozanam's initiative was in part a critique of the utopian socialism of Saint-Simon, itself a response to *laissez-faire* liberalism.) And the signs of the times held good news as well as bad. Thus, in part because Frederic Ozanam asked questions about why people were poor, who benefited from them being poor and what could be done to change their circumstances, he advocated democracy and social protection for workers, believed in a free press and the right of workers to form associations and in fixed wages for regulated working hours. He wanted pensions guaranteed to workers and compensation against unemployment and accidents.

I like to remember this dynamic. It suggests that Catholic social teaching can best be understood broadly: it is not some autochthonous thing, produced in remote Vatican departments, at a level that is so abstractedly universal that it can't be illuminating in very particular historical, social, political or economic circumstances. There may be as much upward and horizontal as there is downward in this dynamic–the developing social teaching emerges out of engagement and connection with dispersed realities 'on the ground' and from reflection on social circumstances in the light of and shaped by the theological/ethical tradition, and in dialogue with society including its intellectual currents. As such, it is never complete, or superseded, though it is established on solid ground. It evolves, in its methodology too, in response to new social and political realities. As a provocation, rather than a system, it poses crucial questions. At least it does when it is not moribund or on the defensive or captured by special interests.

That was not the case with the second document in the canonical tradition, Pius XI's 1931 response to the Great Depression and a development of *Rerum Novarum*—that is, *Quadragesimo Anno (Forty Years Later)*, with its suggestion of a 'third way' between socialism and capitalism. But, there's a sense in which its fate was to be 'captured' in Australia by a movement that had bearing upon the Catholic world in which I grew up. I went to Catholic schools and in my 1960s' secondary school that meant we were being prepared to enter what was perceived as an unsympathetic world: for some there, it was important to arm us with 'a system' to counter other kinds of systems we might encounter. In the aftermath of 'the Split' Catholic social teaching was among the armaments, as it was co-opted by the National Civic Council to whose activists we were introduced. In that period, there was little in the way of dialogue and rather more in the way of polemic, so that ideas proffered by Catholic social teaching became partisan property and in a significant way were dissociated from broader movements of political and social thought and effort. (I believe the distortion this effected is evident in our contemporary public discussion–where the language has been lost to some or is ignored by others.)

In the 1960s those of us who had fathers in the St Vincent de Paul Society may have known about other dimensions, as did any student involved in the YCS movement with its 'See, Judge, Act' methodology. Somewhere in the mix came knowledge about Pope John XXIII's famous social encyclical in 1963, *Pacem in Terris (Peace on Earth)*, just war ideas, corporatist manifestations like the National Catholic Rural Movement, and the Catholic Worker movement and its local offshoots. It was an odd mix of influences and impressions, not at all understood adequately or coherently placed, but strong enough to permeate the consciousness and to leave a deposit of language. I can't recall just when that word *subsidiarity* became part of my personal deposit of language, similarly the '*common good*'–but I do recognise the more recent dating of '*solidarity*'.

Catholic social teaching could never amount to a 'system' though; for one, there is enough tension in it to prevent it working neatly in such a fashion. As I learned along the way, this developing body of teaching orients rather towards justice and *charity*–and suggests a way of life always in community, from the local community to the global. The vocabulary it offers, the reference points it produces (including the not so simple idea that '*Inequality is the root of social evil*', repeated from Francis's *Evangelii Gaudium*[1]), assist in the critical thinking needed to build such a life. Of course it has been much elaborated since the 1960s, including in the way it has repeatedly invited us to reflect on the experiences of people in conditions other than ours and to understand our connections with them.

In my work as a broadcaster I've had opportunities to explore this teaching, invariably in relation to someone else's work. (Bruce Duncan has played a part in this, through his books and contributions to interviews.) I've made programs about Catholic health care and the challenges it faces to be true to its calling (in Australia and in the United States), about the meaning of work and unemployment, about social action in the context of Christian communities, about the St Vincent de Paul Society and its internal work to recover the relationship between charity and justice that its founder articulated. I've had opportunity to observe the effort to use Catholic social teaching as a field of formation for lay leaders of Catholic institutions, the people who have already taken over from religious sisters and brothers the running of schools and hospitals and other institutions, as well as the increasingly diverse people at board levels. Many of them are Catholics, but a significant proportion of the institutional leadership stratum comes from non-Catholic and non-Christian backgrounds. Great effort is being put into this enterprise and I know that another enquiry lies here: how is the enterprise being rewarded in the character and conduct of those institutions? (Indeed, how vitally has the body of Catholic social teaching penetrated the management, employment and social relationships of Church administration itself?) How alive is it in decision-making in all these spheres?

I have seen the vocabulary of Catholic social teaching operate as obstacle, and as open to evasion. The first obstacle is that historical one, of association. But beyond that, key concepts can seem like a rarefied and practically irrelevant argot (as impenetrable for some

---

1. *Evangelii Gaudium: Apostolic Exhortation on the Proclamation of the Gospel in Today's World* (24 November 2013) 202-208. <http://w2.vatican.va/content/francesco/en/apost_exhortations/documents/papa-francesco_esortazione-ap_20131124_evangelii-gaudium.html#_ftn173>. Accessed 6 April 2014.

as the word 'charism'!). Or they can be read as so open and loose as to be wary of being pinned down in 'real life' or in 'real' politics. They can be seen as easily malleable to partisan political purpose, or to management orientation. Or when applied to that 'real life' they can be dismissed as naive, not adequately cognisant of the laws of 'real life', like 'economics'. These are not uncommon reactions, either explicit or implicit.

That's why I like Pope Francis's writing and his living–his life, his gestures, seem as much a part of the canon of social teaching as does his writing. There is a remarkable freedom there that somehow has the effect of breaching conventions of speech and making the person visible in a web of connection. The response to him discovers for us something Marilynne Robinson argues–that people *are* religious, more responsive to the religious than might be otherwise thought, and therefore responsive to Francis's language of mercy and forgiveness and justice. It seems that Pope Francis is enacting that which Ozanam insisted–that the church has an important social role to play in the wider world. The effect in Australia I hope and indeed think is to detach Catholic social teaching from aspects of past association, and to make it more widely suggestive. In an interesting way Francis has made it possible for everyone to have a say. Most of us are no more or less expert than he is in matters of border control, or economic policy or public policy. But Christians are all concerned about justice and charity, about manifestations of evil and the possibility of good–and with the vivid help of Francis Christians can make that reference in the public sphere. They can say what is wrong with the way things are and contribute to a more long-term and constructive dialogue about what might be instead. Those who are expert will of course make their contributions. (The possibilities of such bringing together are evident in efforts now being made to combat human trafficking.)[2] But everyone, including Christians expert and otherwise, has the competence to speak as citizen, and Christians have an obligation born of their faith. The Church's social teaching is an aid to this participation.

---

2. 'Church and Law Enforcement in Partnership', 9-10 April 2014: <http://www.catholic-ew.org.uk/Home/Special-Events/Combating-Human-Trafficking-Rome-Conference>. Accessed 6 April 2014.

As the November 2013 Yarra Institute Conference demonstrated, the business of explaining yourself to a 'stranger' can be both exciting and challenging. It seemed to me, listening to the various contributions, that it was truly revivifying for contributors to return to the foundations of their traditions, in order to orient themselves and their listeners in a discussion of Christian social teaching. For listeners it was stirring to hear people recount what had, essentially, stirred the speakers to the commitments that had led their lives. And every telling, however distinctive its detail, spoke to experiences and challenges shared by members of all the Christian traditions represented.

Each foundation story offered great riches, and provoked questions about what may have gone out of sight in radically different social circumstances from those origin times. Thus, Gerald Rose described the way contemporary social trends in effect give primacy of authority to personal experience and so unbalance the founding equilibrium in the Church of Christ between the authority of biblical tradition, of reason and of personal experience. While a social shift has now occurred towards the authority of personal experience, for the Church the opposite is occurring–authority is to be located in tradition.

Jenny Begent evoked the beginnings of the Salvation Army in Scripture-based conviction of the call to work for justice–social justice and 'kingdom' justice. Its larger purpose was to proclaim the kingdom of God and help people enter into it. As a prophetic tradition in theology and in practice, emphasising the importance of a visible, lived faith, it was at its best when it responded to a tangible social evil. Times have changed and the Salvation Army works within established norms in social service: its challenge now is to hold together its evangelical mission and its social service, and to regain its prophetic voice.

Max Vodola set the Catholic tradition of social teaching against a series of contradictions: problems besetting dialogue within the ecclesial community which prevent or inhibit wider dialogue, the confining very often to bishops and priests of competence to speak out on behalf of the Church, the challenges presented by evident failures to articulate the connection between faith and political practice.

Geoff Pound described the Baptist tradition's foundation in revolt, from which it drew a capacity to speak with prophetic voice, along with a bent towards separatism: the challenge was to bring people together to address the social dimension of 'salvation' as well as the personal.

Mark Zirnsak described the Uniting Church's commitment to social justice flowing out of its foundation documents, its global vision and the constraints presented by limited resources.

Fr Shenouda Boutros spoke of the Coptic Orthodox Church's self-understanding formed by its experience of martyrdom, marginalisation and separation. Its tradition of providing a mutually supportive strong social network has made the transition to Australia, providing for migrants and refugees. Now the task was to conceive of the community in a wider sense. It was also necessary to overcome cultural and generational differences within the Coptic Church communities in Australia.

Ray Cleary described being captivated by Christianity as a young man: Christianity for example had proposed forgiveness and restoration as opposed to revenge. But in a wider social context of 'Christian irrelevance' the Church to which he had been drawn was caught up with survival. While church agencies had maintained a commitment to justice, in a sense social justice had been privatised into those agencies. The task now was to bring distinctively Christian perspectives to the public square, and to develop strategies such as partnership with other voices to enable serious attention to be given these perspectives.

I'd like finally to make three comments about these exchanges at the Yarra Institute Conference. To begin with, I note that for the first time these people from different Christian traditions got together to talk specifically about Christian social teaching, and even to discuss the usefulness of Catholic social teaching in this context. Such an openness to exchange is a gift of this generation of speakers. The second thing to be said is that they were heard by relatively few. The third is that they were heard by fewer still young people.

Therein lie opportunity and a serious challenge. Why is it when social justice is such a part of structures and institutions that a more diverse age cohort cannot be drawn to such a gathering? The gathering was itself a model of diversity—should there not be a commitment to extending this diversity to include younger people? And to determining how this might be achieved? Here I return to Frederic Ozanam—he was 20 and a student when he founded the St Vincent de Paul Society, 23 when he wondered whether society at large 'will be merely a great exploitation for the benefit of the strongest or the dedication of each individual to the good of all and especially to the protection of the weak.'[3]

---

3. Joseph I Dirvin, CM, translator and editor, *Frederic Ozanam: A Life in Letters* (St Louis, MO: Society of Saint Vincent de Paul Council of the United States, 1986) 96-97.

Contributors

Dr John D'Arcy May is formerly Professor Interfaith Dialogue at the Irish School of Ecumenics, Trinity College Dublin, Research Fellow, University of Divinity, Adjunct Professor, Centre for Interreligious Dialogue, Australian Catholic University, and Adjunct Senior Research Fellow, Centre for Studies in Religion and Theology, Monash University.

Professor Frank Brennan SJ is Professor of Law at Australian Catholic University, and Adjunct Professor at the College of Law and the National Centre for Indigenous Studies, Australian National University. He was the founding director of UNIYA, the Jesuit Social Justice Centre in Sydney, and from mid-2014 has taken up a fellowship in the Jesuit Institute at Boston College USA.

Major Jenny Begent has been a Salvation Army officer for 28 years and served in leadership positions in Western Australia, Tasmania and Victoria, with particular concern about homelessness, housing and family violence. She currently provides oversight to Community and Social Services in the Greater Melbourne Area.

Rev Dr Max Vodola lectures in history at Catholic Theological College in Melbourne and is pastor of Flemington/Kensington parishes. His doctoral studies focused on Pope John XXIII and the Second Vatican Council.

Revd Dr Gerald Rose is co-founder of Social Justice Networks of Churches of Christ in Vic/Tas. He has ministered in churches in South

Australia, New Zealand and Victoria as well as serving as Director of Conference Departments in Australia and the USA, and as President of the Vic/Tas Conference. Recently he was Minister (part-time) at Mulgrave Church of Christ. He has specialised in the sociology of religion and shifts in western culture.

Revd Dr Geoff Pound has served in Baptist parishes in New Zealand and Victoria in various roles, including Home Mission Superintendent, Director of Leadership Training, President of the Baptist Union of Victoria and Principal of Whitley College. He is currently senior pastor of the Ashburton Baptist Church.

Revd Dr Ray Cleary has been chair of Anglicare Australia, and for ten years its Chief Executive Officer before becoming Director of Ministry Formation and Sambell Lecturer in Pastoral and Practical Theology at Trinity College, University of Divinity in Melbourne.

Dr Mark Zirnsak is the Director of the Justice & International Mission, Synod of Victoria and Tasmania, Uniting Church in Australia.

Rev Fr Shenouda Boutros is parish priest at St Bishoy & St Shenouda Coptic Orthodox Church in Bulleen Victoria. He is a council member and chaplain of the St Athanasius Coptic Orthodox Theological College, and also a chaplain at La Trobe University. He was a proxy delegate for the Coptic Orthodox Church to the World Council of Churches Faith and Order Commission in 2012.

Margaret Coffey has worked for the ABC as a broadcaster for many years, chiefly producing feature programs for the *Encounter* series. She investigates in the Australian context and more widely the worldviews and religious experience of different faith traditions, both historically and in the present day.

ATF Press Style Guide

1. Indented material: Indented quotations, of over 5 lines of material, or 30 words, should be indented on both sides. There should be a space of one line before and after the quotation. Quotations should not have quotation marks at the beginning or end and within the quotation there should be single quotation marks (exception: where *within* the indented quote there is a quote that is also quoting (. . . ' . . . " . . . " . . ' . . .).

2. Headings: Headings should not be numbered unless there is a particular need (for example, cross-referencing within the text, scientific or text-book style presentation. Capitals should be used for the initial letters only of headings and subsections (unless using proper nouns). Headings and subsections do not have punctuation at the end. (

3. Spelling: The general guide to spelling will be taken from *The Macquarie Dictionary*. We use '-ise' forms for words (and not '-ize') (so: realise, globalisation, modernise . . .). Hyphens should be used in words such as 'co-operate' and 'co-ordinate', except where the mathematical 'coordinate' is used. *The Australian Writers Dictionary* is a valuable tool for assisting with the use of hyphens. We prefer World War 1 (and not First World War). All Latin, Greek and all foreign words should be in italics and have an English translation. We prefer transliterations of biblical languages but if biblical languages are used then the English must be given in brackets.

4. Abbreviations and contractions
Abbreviations are generally not used: editor (rather than ed.), translated by (rather than trans.), volume (rather than vol.), number (rather than no.), for example (not e.g.). Those such as USA or UN do not have full points between the letters. Contractions, which end in the last of the whole word, should not be given a full point: Dr (Doctor), St (Saint).

5. *Personal initials* Do not insert a stop or space between personal initials, as for example: AN Simple.

6. *Dates and numbers* Avoid unnecessary punctuation: 24 June 1999 (and not 24 June, 1999, or June 24th, 1999). 1990s (not 1990's). Twentieth century (not 20th century). When referring to the age of a person, 'she was in her eighties', use the spelt-out form, but use figures in the hyphenated form when writing of an '80-year-old woman'. In text use of year span: 1991–8 with an en rule (not hyphen and no space) (not 1991-8), 1902–3 (and not1902-03), 1878–83. When in headings or subsections, use 1990–1992. Financial years are 1991/92. Spans of numbers: use as few digits as possible, with the exception of 11–19, where 1 is repeated. So: 112–13, 103–8, 34–9, 145–53. Numbers up to ninety-nine are spelt out in the text, except where figures are needed in a string of hyphenated words (35-hour week) or where figures will assist with clarity (when several numbers are compared). Numbers over ninety-nine are usually written in numerals but can be spelt out (about a thousand people) where figures seem inappropriate in the text. When a date is the first word of the sentence, use the spelt out form. Use figures for sums of money, $1.24, but three cents. Times should be in words rather than numerals when precision is not intended. So: 'They had to leave at three o'clock'. But where a precise time is intended: 'The bus leaves at 10.23am'. Percentages should be spelt out in the text: ninety-three per cent (note 'per cent'). But 93% in footnotes and tables.

7. *Hyphens and dashes*: En rules (a short dash) should be used for spans of numbers: 182–3; for Christian biblical references for the verses: Mk 3:12–13; for expressions of time: May–June; expressions of distance: Adelaide–Melbourne; and where 'and' is meant. Em rules (a long dash) are used in parenthetical statements, with no gap either side. For example, 'To have wide lawns—and not any garden—is not necessary for a happy life'.

8. *Quotations*: Indented quotes do not have opening and closing quotation marks. Short extracts of less than 5 lines (or 30 words) may appear within the text, enclosed in single quotation marks. Quotation marks should go inside the final full point if there is any authorial

comment within the sentence; that is, the full point belongs to the author as part of her/his sentence. Time and time again, 'people do not speak' was quoted by authors. Or Sally was known to have said that 'the weather at the Cape is fine all year round'. If the quotation begins within a sentence containing authorial comment but runs to more than one sentence, it is acceptable to place the closing quotation mark after the final full point. George Stephens wrote with glee 'about fifty men broke out of the prison yesterday evening. We expect to have them rounded up before the week is past.' When a sentence is entirely quoted material, then all punctuation belongs to the quotation; therefore, the final full point goes inside the closing quotation mark. Mary received the telegram at 10 am. 'I never knew a darker moment than when I read of John's death.' Double quotation marks are only used for quotes within quotes. Eggs were thrown at the 'vote "No" for a republic' banner.

Indicate any omission from a quotation by the use of an ellipsis (. . .), with a single space keyed in before and after each point. Do not insert an additional full point if the ellipsis occurs at the end of a sentence. Do not use editorial caps within square brackets as in '[I]t is then . . .', but leave the lower close letter, or adjust the way the quote is used.

9. Footnotes

Notes should be used for sources you have used, published or unpublished, to a brief discussion of the sources, to develop a point out of the text, or to cross reference to other parts of the text. Footnotes in the text should be used as a superscript text and in Times.

9.1 Books: First name (not initials) and surname, title of the book (in italics), place of publication, publisher and year (all in brackets), followed by page numbers. We do not use p or pp for footnote entries or in the text. In the text write word 'page' if necessary. In footnotes there is minimal punctuation: First reference:

Victor Pfitzner, *The Islands of Peru* (Adelaide: ATF Press, 1999), 21.

Second and subsequent references copy and paste name (surname only) and title of book (or abbreviated title), followed by page number. Where a title is long a suitable shorter version should be used in second and subsequent references.

Pfitzner, *The Islands of Peru*, 28.

9.2 Articles in journals: First name, surname, title of article, (with single inverted commas), title of the journal (in italics), volume and number, year (year in brackets), followed by a colon and then the pages of the article. We do not uses p or pp in footnotes or in the text. First reference: Victor Pfitzner, 'Where To From Here?', in *Interface: A Pyschology Review*, 1/2 (1998): 22–3.

Second and subsequent references: Pfitzner, 'Where to From Here?', 38.

9.3 Articles in books: First name, surname, title of article (with single inverted commas), edited by, with first name first, title of the book (in italics), place of publication, publisher and year (all in brackets), followed by a colon and then page. Victor Pfitzner, 'Yesterday, Today And Tomorrow', in *Readings in Contemporary History*, edited by Victor Pfitzner (Adelaide: ATF Press, 2002), 22–56. *9.4 Web references*: First name, surname, title of article, web address enclosed in <…>, access date. Victor Pfitzner, 'Today and Not Tomorrow' at <www.newspoll.com.apost-au>. Accessed 20 July 2010. (No underlining).

10. Bibliography: We do not normally have a bibliography included with texts. But if one is to be used then, authors surname first, followed by initials and in alphabetical order of surname. Title of the book is in italics and with place of publisher, publisher and year in brackets. Pfitzner, V, *History of The New Time* (Adelaide: ATF Press, 2002).